Yoking Up with Jesus and the Kingdom of God Government

By

James L. Monteria

CLM Publications & Publishing, LLC
P.O. Box 932, Chesterfield, VA 23832

All rights reserved. No part of this book may be reproduced without written permission from the publisher, except for use of brief review for the furthering of the Kingdom of God unless otherwise indicated; all Scriptures are taken from the King James Version of the Bible

Yoking Up with Jesus and the Kingdom of God Government

All rights reserved. No part of this book may be reproduced without written permission from the publisher, except for use of brief review for the furthering of the Kingdom of God unless otherwise indicated; all Scriptures are taken from the King James Version of the Bible

CLM Publications & Publishing, LLC
P.O. Box 932
Chesterfield, VA 23832
www.clmpublication.info
ISBN: 978-0-9821450-9-8

Cover Design/Graphics: Shelly E. Middleton
Author: James L. Monteria
Associate Editor: Sandra Alexandra
Published by CLM Publications & Publishing, LLC

Copyright © 2013 by CLM Publications & Publishing, LLC Printed in the United States of America; All rights reserved under International Copyright Law. Contents and cover may not be reproduced in whole or in part in any form without the expressed written consent of the publisher.

Section I, *we want to introduce you to the kingdom of God, which is the Government of God.*

Introduction Page 1

Chapter 1 Location of the Kingdom of God on earth Page 11
Chapter 2 Heavenly means of Communication Page 22
Chapter 3 How to know if you are operating in
the Kingdom of God Page 32

Section II, *we want to establish that every Kingdom has a constitution that the citizens must adhere to if they want to be a lawful citizen within the kingdom.*

Chapter 4 The Constitution of the Kingdom of God Page 43

Section III, *we listed some of the steps and laws by which we are to take and apply to our lives if we want to enter into the Kingdom of God and enjoy the benefits of being a citizen of the Kingdom of God.*

Chapter 5 The Laws of Salvation Page 48
Chapter 6 The Baptism of the Holy Spirit Page 59
Chapter 7 The Royal Law of the Kingdom (Agape) Love Page 72
Chapter 8 The Law of Forgiveness Page 83
Chapter 9 Faithfulness and Consistency Page 93
Chapter 10 The Law of Meditation Page 100
Chapter 11 The Law of Faith Page 112
Chapter 12 The Law of Tithing Page 125
Chapter 13 The Law of Sowing and Reaping Page 140
Chapter 14 The Law of Favor Page 147
Chapter 15 The Law of Confession Page 160
Chapter 16 Sample Prayer of Agreement Page 175
Chapter 17 Sample Prayer of Faith (Finances) Page 181
Chapter 18 Naming Your Seed Page 185
Chapter 19 Tracking your Seed Page 191
Chapter 20 Yoking up with Jesus and the Kingdom
of God Government Page 197
Decision Pages Page 205
Endnotes Page 209
About the Author Page 210

Acknowledgement

First, and foremost, I would not even know God, or be able to write anything about Him, were it not for His grace and mercy! I have come to appreciate the grace of God, the Lordship of Jesus Christ, and the Holy Spirit's presence in my life and my ministry, even more than words could express.

Foreword

Come and Learn of Me - The message of Jesus, according to Matthew 11:28-30 states that Jesus said, "Come unto me, all ye that labor and are heavy laden, and I will give you rest. Take my yoke upon you, and learn of me; for I am meek and lowly in heart: and ye shall rest unto your souls. "For my yoke is easy, and my burden is light." There are many basic benefits that belong to us as Christians. Many Christians have a very limited understanding of Salvation, and that is limited to eternal life. For many Christians, eternal life is what they look forward to when they depart from this world into eternity. In studying the Word of God, eternal life begins the moment you are saved, and there are many benefits of salvation that are to be enjoyed now as part of our daily lifestyle. Also, the function of a kingdom is new to most of us because we are born into a country under a democratic system form of government.

Jesus said…
Take My Yoke upon you and Learn of Me

I give unto the <u>Keys to the Kingdom of God</u>... referred to the laws, and principle by which the Kingdom of God operates.

Jesus said… Matthew 16:18-19 "And I also say to you that you are Peter, and on this rock I will build **My church**, and the gates of Hades shall not prevail against it. 19 "And I will give you the keys of the kingdom of heaven, and whatever you bind on earth will be bound in heaven, and whatever you loose on earth will be loosed in heaven."

In the next few chapters, we will share with a combination of Laws and Principles that one needs to be knowledge of, and really understand to the point that they are applying to one life and get the results that is promised.

Yoking Up with Jesus and the Kingdom of God Government

Laws and Principles

Laws and Principles establish the criteria and regulations fixed by the King himself, by which his Kingdom will serve and administered.

The laws of a kingdom are the means by which one ensured or guarantee of the benefits of the King in His Kingdom.

The citizens cannot alter laws in a kingdom, nor are they subject to a citizen referendum or debate. Plainly put, the word of the King is law in His Kingdom. When the laws of the Government of God are violated the blessing stop.

<u>The Laws that are mention in this book are not referring to the laws of the Old Testament and New Testament, but the LAWS of the Kingdom of God Government.</u>

Purpose of this Book!

Hello, Author James L. Monteria, in my Christian life I found that there are times when everything I did, everything I touch was blessed. This has happened many times in my life, but I wonder why these blessings stop.

You know in the Holy Bible, **Hebrews 13:8 says...**"Jesus Christ the same yesterday, and today, and forever." That means that God change not. In my research, and I discovered that in the kingdom of God, there is the Government of God, and within the Government of God, there are laws, and when we walk in line with these laws we are blessed, but when we walk contrary to these laws the blessing stop.

WHY? There are limitations within the laws of God, where God is able to bless us and outside of these laws, He will not bless us. I remember reading a book where the Lord spoke to a person and said, "I bless all of my people as far as I can. Do you know that something as simple as a bad attitude can block your blessing?

Think of it from this perspective, in the United States, we have a government; there are laws by which we are to drive. If we follow these laws, it will keep us from getting a ticket, from the possibility of accident, and or even death.

In order to operate within the laws of the Government of God, we must know the laws of the Government of God.

Section I

In this section, we want to introduce you to the kingdom of God, which is the Government of God.

Yoking Up with Jesus and the Kingdom of God's Government

Introduction

In this book, *Yoking Up with Jesus and the Kingdom of God's Government*, I am thankful for the significant amount of teaching and preaching pertaining to the Kingdom of God and its style of government. The fundamental purpose of this book is to give you a clearer understanding of the Kingdom of God and its divine government. Within the 4 gospels and Acts chapter 1, the phrase Kingdom of Heaven occurs 112 times, the phrase Kingdom of God occurs 204 times and the kingdom of darkness occurs 12 times.

I will also share with you some of its laws and principles and how to apply them. When we think of the kingdom of God, it refers to lordship, dominion and King Jesus.

Everywhere Jesus went he preached about the Kingdom of God starting from Matthew 4:17 and concluding with Acts 1:1-3; where Jesus for forty days instructed the apostles of things pertaining to the Kingdom of God, which was his assignment.

His message was not primarily focus on that you must be born again, however He did say that you will not see the Kingdom of God except you be born again according to John 3:3. Neither did He make these other subjects the focus of His preaching: prosperity, healing, the baptism of the Holy Spirit, or many the other subjects that are being preached so much about today.

Jesus taught about those things, and He demonstrated them in His day-by-day ministry, but He did not preach them.

There is a big difference. Jesus had only one message: the Kingdom of God. That was His assignment, and He passed it on to us. His assignment is our assignment. It would have been great to get saved and go straight to Heaven, but He left us here on the earth in order to complete the work that He began.

He sits on the throne of heaven directing that work through His representatives. Unfortunately, most of us do not really understand what Jesus meant when He spoke of the Kingdom."

1. Here in the United States, we have or allegedly have a democratic system of government where elections allow us to choose a candidate for office in an organization by casting ballots chosen by the voters and citizens.

2. The Middle East is governed by dictatorship. This is a tyranny style of government (as known as an authoritarian government) that identifies a person who has absolute power and control over that country.

3. In Europe, the United Kingdom of Great Britain, they have:

   - Kings and Queens, who are descendants of Royal parents.

   - The Prime Minister is the Chief member of the cabinet of ministry with a parliamentary system.

   - House of Lords

   - House of Commons

In the above list of examples of government and/or kingdoms, do not apply to God's divine standards of administration. When you think about the kingdom, it is synonymous to a government. However, in this lesson we are talking about the kingdom of God and His divine government.

I come to recognize that there are several groups of people in the world today. The heathens (sinners), the religious (have their way of getting to God), but for the citizens of the kingdom of God, and those who are serious about their citizenship in the Kingdom of God. This lesson is for them. The sincere citizens of the Kingdom of God (*In Paul's writing 2 Corinthians 2:17*)

1. What is the Kingdom of Heaven? It is the spiritual home of God or the Presence of God, the 3rd heaven According to Isaiah 66:1 Acts 7:49; ..." Heaven is my throne, and earth is my footstool"; and Revelation 4:1-8; It is the place where those that are Born again will go when life here on the earth is over.

In the kingdom of Heaven, God has nine categories of Angels: Angels, Archangels, Cherubims, and Seraphims.

We must understand that the Kingdom of Heaven is a real place, a prepare place for a prepared people, and The Kingdom of God is the Government of God, the system by which He operates. Many times, especially here in the United States of America, we are not familiar with the functionality of a kingdom system of government, but are more familiar with a democratic system of government.

2. What is the Kingdom of God? It is the invisible divine government located in the spirit realm that is established on the earth when the will of its King has been carried out (*Isaiah9:6*). "

3. What is the kingdom of darkness? The Kingdom of darkness Head Quarters is located in the 2nd heaven, In addition, there is the Kingdom of Darkness, that has a kingdom system of government, and we as believers should not be ignorant of that system. Satan is their leader, and in the kingdom of darkness, satan has five categories of fallen Angels: Principalities, powers, rulers of the darkness of this world, spiritual wickedness in high places, and demons. In addition the kingdom of darkness has principalities ruler ship over His Kingdoms of the earth, such as Financial, Economical, Religious, Political, Media, Arts & theater, and Social.

> Matthew 4:8; but in Revelation 11:15; We see that the kingdoms of the world will become the kingdom of our Lord.

Two Kingdoms (Governmental systems) on planet earth

Initially, we had the kingdom of God, God created a planet called earth. Earth is the extension of heaven, or a child of heaven. One is in the spiritual realm and the other is in the natural realm, or spirit being with a natural body.

Within the Kingdom of Heaven, there was a rebellion by one of God's angels by the name of lucifer. He was an anointed cherub who evidently had some type of throne and authority. Lucifer decided that he wanted to be more powerful than God who created him.

The results of this rebellion caused Lucifer and one-third of God's angels that followed him to be kicked out of heaven causing the creation of the kingdom of darkness. Once Adam sinned through disobedience, he caused the earth to come under the ruler ship of Satan. In order to understand the seriousness of what Adam did, he became a servant of Satan, and Satan became his father. To take this a little deeper as we must understand the scriptures, at this present time, we have two kingdoms on one planet:

1. The kingdom of God with a divine governmental system of laws and principles based on Giving and Receiving (*See Matthew 4:17*).

2. The kingdom of darkness, the devil and his debacle governmental system of laws and principles based on Buying and Selling which is also known as the Babylon system. (*See Matthew 12:22-26*)

The kingdom of darkness is an invisible evil government in the spiritual realm that is established on the earth by satan. Satan, who perverts what he took from Adam now is the head. When a person habitually practices sin, they are operating in Satan's government, the kingdom of darkness. *Revelation 11:15*

In examining the Holy Scriptures, Ephesians 1:21, 3:10 and Colossians 2:10; 15; we will clearly see that Jesus operating as a man defeated satan according to 1 John 3:8.

In the Kingdom of darkness, the devil with his host has 5 categories of fallen Angels: principalities, powers of the air, rulers of the darkness of this world, and spiritual wickedness in the Heavenlies, and demons."

Doctor Luke primary wrote about this in the books of Luke and Acts. We find in the books of Acts that Philip and Paul preached and taught the Kingdom of God.

- **Acts 8:11-13;** Philip preached **the Kingdom of God**
- **Acts 19:7-9;** Paul preached **the Kingdom of God**
- **Acts 28:30-31;** Paul preached **the Kingdom of God**

According to *Colossians 1:13*; the only way into the kingdom of God and to experience the kingdom life is to be born into it. When the Bible says we must be born again, the original Greek version states that we must be born from above. We are actually born from heaven another government, the divine government/the kingdom of God.

Translated into God's Kingdom

We come into the kingdom of God, and at the same time, the kingdom of God comes inside of us. As believers, we have the kingdom of God on the inside of us. (Luke 17:21; Romans 8:11; Colossians 1:9-14; Ephesians 1:16-18;)

In other words, Jesus was explaining how you should not operate from both kingdoms, while also declaring that the Kingdom of God or the government of God, which is invisible to the natural eyes. Just as Jesus understood this, we need to understand what is going on in the earth is not about people or money, it is about kingdoms and how they are governed.

As the Holy Spirit is governing body of Christ, we need to understand that the church is a living organism and not a building with four walls.

The true believers within the walls are the "called out ones", (Greek word Ecclesia). We have executive leaders such as Apostles, Prophets, Evangelists, Pastors and Teachers. These leaders receive instructions from headquarters, where the Lord Jesus Christ is seated at the right-hand of the throne of God in Heaven via the Holy Spirit.

These executive leaders then impart revelation of knowledge received from Heaven to the citizens of the Kingdom of Heaven by preaching and teaching via the Holy Spirit.

In addition, an individual can receive confirmation of what they have received, because an individual can receive from headquarters just as the executive leaders can via the person of the Holy Spirit. This impartation and confirmation helps us to be effective citizens of the Kingdom of God.

As the co-labor of the body of Christ, we the citizens of the Kingdom of Heaven, we come together in Kingdom business and the purpose is threefold:

1. To bestow upon our God, our King and the Holy Spirit praise and worship that the Godhead is so worthy to receive, thus creating an atmosphere

2. To receive specific instructions about Kingdom operations for this embassy to carry out

3. As ambassadors of the Kingdom of God, we receive instructions and directions, then we are to examine the constitution to see if what we have received is in line with the Word of God

As the citizens Kingdom of God, we are too disseminated to each of our jurisdiction their (place of influence) executing these instructions and directions as examples consequently of being effective kingdom citizens through our living Kingdom of God life.

This is similar to the government of the United States. We have elected official that comes from each state to a central location (Washington, DC) to conduct government business such as making laws on the behalf of the citizens. Then these elected officials will go back to his/her district, state or jurisdiction that they represent and inform them of the laws that have been made.

An Overview of Jesus Ministry

1. Jesus *announced* the arrival of the Kingdom of Heaven is at hand (Matthew 4:17);

2. Jesus explains how we can enter the Kingdom of God. (John 3:3-7, Romans 10:9-10)

3. Jesus preached and taught about the kingdom of God, and its *location* (Luke 17:21) for three years prior to His death, burial and resurrection.

4. Jesus taught about the person of whom is our (Helper, Comforter, Teacher Spirit of Truth, convicts, revels) the Holy Spirit and what He would do when He came after Jesus departed from the earth. (John 14:16-17, 14:26, 16:13).

5. Jesus taught about the kingdom of God for forty days prior to his accession to Heaven (Acts 1:1-3).

6. Paul in His letter to the Thessalonians defined the makeup of humanity. (1 Thessalonians 5:23).

In His letters to the Romans taught us how to be led by the Holy Spirit (Romans 8:14). Paul in His letter to the Philippians on how to know when you are operating in the Kingdom of God (Philippians 4:6-7)

The kingdom of God's is not of this world, but it works on this earth because He put it inside of us. While sojourning here on this earth, Jesus taught extensively about the kingdom of God.

Summary

Jesus has returned to Heaven after completing his responsibility of restoring the kingdom of God back on earth. In restoring the Kingdom back on earth, He raised up disciples and Apostle to continue the preaching of the Gospel of the Kingdom of God or the government of God.

As ambassadors of Christ, we should be concerned only with the interests of our King. Everything we say and do should reflect that desire and that purpose. Our personal opinion does not matter. It is completely improper for an ambassador to express his or her personal opinions while acting in his official capacity as the representative and voice of his government.

As members of the body of Christ, we are the hands, feet, the arms, the fingers of God the earth today, and we are commission to continue what has started.

Chapter One
Location of the Kingdom of God on earth!

In this chapter we want to examine the scriptures to search the location of the Kingdom of God on the earth. Jesus said according to Luke 17:20; "And when he was demanded of the Pharisees, when the kingdom of God should come, he answered them and said, The kingdom of God cometh not with <u>observation</u>:". This means that the Kingdom of God cannot be seen with the natural eye, but the Kingdom of God is very visible in the spiritual realm which is invisible to the natural eyes.

Paul said, according to Romans 14:17; "$_{17}$ For the kingdom of God is not meat and drink; but righteousness, and peace, and joy in the Holy Ghost."

Jesus was once asked when the kingdom of God would come. The kingdom of God, Jesus replied, is not something people will be able to see and point to. He then spoke these striking words: "Neither shall they say, Lo here! or, lo there! for, behold, the kingdom of God is within you." (Luke 17:21) With these words, Jesus gave a voice to teaching that is universal and timeless. Look into every great religious, spiritual, and wisdom tradition and we will find the same precept — that life's ultimate truth is its ultimate treasure, lies within us.

As Jesus made it unambiguously clear, we can experience this inner treasure — and no experience could be more valuable. "But seek ye first the kingdom of God and His righteousness," he declared, "and all these things shall be added unto you" (Matthew 6:33).

From this interior truth of life, he is saying, we will gain all that is needed. Again, Jesus said in Luke 17:20-21; *"*"The kingdom of God does not come with observation; (but by REVELATION) nor will they say, 'See here!' or 'See there!' For indeed, the kingdom of God is within you" (*Emphases added*)

To help us in locating the Kingdom of God on earth, we must understand the makeup of mankind.

Defined the makeup of mankind:

Threefold Nature of Man: Spirit, Soul, and Body

We are taught to think of ourselves in the same way the Bible states. We are a spirit being who possesses a soul and lives in a body. My spirit is the part of me that was born again. This is where God dwells within us. Therefore, I have the nature of God within me. It is the part of me that desires to live right.

I. Man's First dimension - the Spirit

Man is a spirit and that is the part of him that knows God. He dwells in the same class with God. God is a spirit and man is a spirit, and God has made mankind to have fellowship with Him. In Hebrew 4:12, 13; the separation of the threefold nature of man; In 1 Thessalonians 5:23; the makeup of man 2 Kings 6:12-17 Lord opened his eyes. In John 3:7; the rebirth of the human spirit Romans 2:28-29; the spirit of man is the heart of man. 1 Corinthians 14:14, 18; The Spirit of man prayeth.

God made man for his own pleasure. Man is not an animal. In order to have fellowship with God, man must be in the same category with God. Therefore, just as God is Spirit, so is man a spirit according to John 4:24. We cannot know God or touch him physically.

He is not a man; instead, He is Spirit. We cannot communicate with God mentally, for He is a Spirit, and it is through our spirit that we come to know God. So we know that God is a Spirit and yet God, who is a spirit, took upon Himself a man's body.

Jesus was God manifested in the flesh. In John 1:1-3, 14; and Luke 16:19-31 The story of Lazarus and the rich man, and in Ezekiel 36:26-27 Promises of a new Heart. Also see 2 Corinthians 5:17-21; and 2 Corinthians 5:6-8.

Living in this natural and physical world as we do, it is difficult to realize that the spirit world is more real to us than this natural world that we live in. When people think about their existence, they only think of their physical bodies, and when they are dead they no longer exist.

However, the above scriptures tell us that the real man is the inward man. , The hidden man of the heart is an eternal being. He will live on long after his "earthly house" has returned to the dust. My spirit has a voice and we call that voice our 'conscience,' as I walk according to the Word of God, it is by my spirit that God will lead, guide and direct me according to Romans 8:14. (See Proverbs 20:27).

II Man's Second Dimension - The Soul

Let us look more closely now into the second part of man's three fold nature - the Soul. The soul of man is the part that contains our emotion, mind, and will. It is the part of us that deals with the reasoning, mental state of man.

According to Romans 12:2, God is not going to do anything with our body or our mind. God contacts our spirit. We contact God with our spirit (the inward man or the hidden man of the heart) to become a new man in Christ. Now it is up to you and I to do something with our mind.

The battle for the Christian lays in the mind, which is the soulish part of man. This is the area of attack because it is where a man makes a choice. Reason is the voice of the soul. If we are not careful we reason ourselves out of the will of God.

We are to be mindful that the scripture of the Lord invites us to come and reason together. When we first get born again, our flesh carries the bulk of the weight. After growing spiritually the spirit starts pulling more of that weight. The decision making element that is often caught in the middle, is our soul which contain our mind, will, and emotions).

We decide what we will do and we make our own choices. For this reason alone is why we must feed the Word of God into our minds. We must 'restore our souls.' If the mind does not have an understanding of the Bible, it will always go with the flesh. When we put the Word of God in us it will completely drive out all things that are contrary to the will of God. Start saying to yourself: I am a spirit, I have a soul, and I live in a physical body. My mind is renewed and my body is subdued.

Paul said we need according to Romans 12:1-2;

1) Do something with our bodies - "present your bodies a living sacrifice"
2) Do something with our minds – "be ye transformed by the renewing of your Mind"

God has given us his word and we are supposed to feed upon that word. This will renew our minds. However, He also put teachers in the church to renew our minds and to bring us the revelation of the kingdom of God's words. So our mind is renewed by two methods: Feeding upon God's word in our own private time through study and meditation.

3) Being taught by the Holy Spirit via anointed teachers in James 1:21 and Psalm 23:3 it shows the way we can grow in strength and knowledge of the word, and we can walk in its light as our minds are renewed daily with the word of God.

III Man's Third Dimension - The Body

Let us look now at what the scripture has to say about our bodies. As we have said, man's spirit is the inward man the part of him that knows God.

The body is the outward man, the physical house that we live in. Our body has a voice and we call that voice a 'feeling.' Our body is the physical suit (or house) that we live in while we are on this earth.

If we go by our feelings we will get into a lot of trouble, for satan is the god of this world system according to 2 Corinthians 4:4; and if we let our bodies dominate our feelings, he can and will gain entrance into our lives. It makes no difference if we feel like it or not. We do what God tells us to do in His Word.

The body itself is not evil, but it can and will be used for evil. We are the ones who control it. If we allow our bodies to control us, we are letting our flesh rule. The flesh has been defined as the sinful nature, the lower nature, the old nature, the selfish nature, the human nature, the carnal nature, and the old self. To sum it all up, the flesh is the sinful desires or feelings that a person can have, saved or unsaved!

You may think that you can never control your flesh, but you can in accordance with Romans 6:14. Jesus died on the cross for our sins. So we must nail ourselves to the same cross and be crucified with Christ according to Galatians 2:20. In 1 Corinthians 9:27; it is clear that the choice is ours.

We can let our body continue to dominate us if we want, but there will always be a price to pay because of this decision the body if we let it, will want to go on doing the things that it has always done. On the other hand, we can choose to keep our body under control. Our inward man can dominate it and present it to God as a living sacrifice.

In Romans 12:1, He said for us to do something with our bodies to "present your bodies a living sacrifice...." It is up to us if we don't do anything with our bodies; nothing will be done with them. In Romans 1:17, Paul is not writing to sinners, but to believers.

According to 1 Corinthians 6:19; "What Know ye not that your body is the temple of the Holy Ghost which is in you, which ye have of God, and ye are not your own?" In examining the Tabernacle in the Old Testament you that the components or compartments of the Tabernacle was the outer court, the Inner court, and the Holy of Holies. Now in comparison to the makeup of mankind; our body is the outer court, our soul is the inner court, and our spirit is the holy of holies. The Holy Spirit is within the spirit of citizens (believers) of the Kingdom of God. The Holy Spirit who is the third member of the Godhead is who lead us and reveal things pertaining to the Kingdom of God.

According to 2 Corinthians 5:17; the body is not new; however, at the coming of Christ we will have a new body. Right now God expects us to do something with our bodies.

As we have shared with you from the word of God concerning the threefold nature of man, we are the decision-makers. We decide what we will or will not do. Let us decide to let Christ rule. Let us be victorious, be overcomers, and be spirit-led believers in every area of life. Amen.

Walking in the Spirit, Galatians 5:22-23 states; these are the characteristics that should be in your life (which shows what kingdom principles and guidelines you are operating by): love, joy, peace, long-suffering, gentleness, goodness, faith, meekness, and temperance.

The realm of this world (the natural) and satan deal with us through the lust of our flesh walking after the lust of the frame, according to Galatians 5:19-22;

> "Now the works of the flesh are manifest, which are *these;* adultery, fornication, uncleanness, lasciviousness, 20 Idolatry, witchcraft, hatred, variance, emulations, wrath, strife, seditions, heresies, 21 Envyings, murders, drunken- ness, revellings, and such like: of the which I tell you before, as I have also told *you* in time past, that they which do such things shall not inherit the kingdom of God."

These are the characteristics that should not be in your spirit (which show what kingdom principles and guidelines you are operating by): adultery, adultery, uncleanness, lasciviousness, idolatry, witchcraft, hatred, variance, emulations, wrath, strife, seditions, heresies, envying, murders, alcohol addiction, and reveling.

One final important note: satan through his wicked devices and his realm is out to destroy human beings simply because man is the conception of God and he, the devil finds pleasure in destroying what God has made. For everything that God has, satan has a counterfeit or he has perverted what God has created. Now we can understand what Paul was saying in writing to the Galatians in 5:16-25.

"*This* I say then, Walk in the Spirit, and ye shall not fulfill the lust of the flesh. 17 For the flesh lusteth against the Spirit, and the Spirit against the flesh: and these are contrary the one to the other: so that ye cannot do the things that ye would. 18 But if ye be led of the Spirit, ye are not under the law. 19 Now the works of the flesh are manifest, which are *these*; Adultery, fornication, uncleanness, lasciviousness, 20 Idolatry, witchcraft, hatred, variance, emulations, wrath, strife, seditions, heresies, 21 Envyings, murders, drunkenness, revellings, and such like: of the which I tell you before, as I have also told *you* in time past, that they which do such things shall not inherit the kingdom of God. 22 But the fruit of the Spirit is love, joy, peace, long-suffering, gentleness, goodness, faith. Galatians in 5:16-25;

Again walking in the Spirit, in Galatians 5:22-23; these are the characteristics that should be in your life (which shows what kingdom principles and guidelines you are operating by): love, joy, peace, long-suffering, gentleness, goodness, faith, meekness, and temperance.

The kingdom of this world (the natural) and satan deal with us through the lust of our flesh walking after the lust of the flesh, according to Galatians 5:19-22.

In Ephesians 1:16-18; "do not cease to give thanks for you, making mention of you in my prayers: 17 that the God of our Lord Jesus Christ, the Father of glory, may give to you the spirit of wisdom and revelation in the knowledge of Him, 18 the eyes of your understanding being enlightened; that you may know what is the hope of His calling, what are the riches of the glory of His inheritance in the saints."

We need to really understanding of whom we are and what we have been blessed with, and the true comprehension come through real mediation on these scriptures verses and allowing the Holy Spirit reveal give revelation of who you and what you have been blessed with.

Jesus said in **Luke 17:21,** that the Kingdom of God is within you, is defined here in **Romans 8:11;** *"But if the Spirit of Him who raised Jesus from the dead dwells in you, He who raised Christ from the dead will also give life to your mortal bodies through His Spirit who dwells in you."*

Again, Jesus in John 14:16, 17 and 26 defined the role of the person of the Holy Spirit in the life of the believers, and we have clarified in Romans 8:14-16; *"For as many as are led by the Spirit of God, they are the sons of God. ^{15} For ye have not received the spirit of bondage again to fear; but ye have <u>received the Spirit</u> of adoption, whereby we cry, Abba, Father. ^{16} The Spirit itself <u>beareth witness</u> with our spirit, that we are the children of God:"*

When you get born-again, you become a new creation in Christ, according to 2 Corinthians 5:17-21; and this includes a new heart.

1. Listen to Your Heart.

Paul did not say, "The Lord told me" that this voyage will be with much hurt and damage. He simply said, "I perceive" that it will. In his spirit, Paul had an inward perception, inward premonition, and an inward witness that the voyage would be dangerous. This is the main way God leads all of us. Paul did not perceive this physically. In his spirit he had a witness. Acts 27:9-10 (NKJV)

Summary

The Holy Spirit abides in our spirits. That is why our heart knows things our brain does not know. But we have not been taught to listen to our spirits, and sometimes we are reluctant to do so.

Spirit-filled believers continually miss it, make mistakes, and fail is because our spirits which should guide us are kept locked away in prison, so to speak. Knowledge, or intellect, has taken the throne. Any person who shuts his spirit off and never listens to it – because the heart of human being is the candle of the Lord become crippled in spirit. Proverbs 20:27;

If you are a citizen of the Kingdom of God, a born again believer, the Kingdom is within your heart. I heard this illustration in identifying the location of God; most of us have a desk top computer and a cell phone, and we think of God has a desk top, when God in us is like have a cell phone.

Chapter Two
Heavenly means of Communication

In this chapter we will examine scriptures references that pertain to Heavenly Communication system. Over the years of being a Christian I have purposely set my heart to obey the Word of God and the Spirit of God. As I continue my study of "In understanding the Kingdom of God, and especially the subject of Heaven, I have found it to be so rewarding that God loves us beyond our wildest imaginations. Even the various means of communication are so cool. The very first miracle that Jesus performed was the miracle of pleasure by turning the water into wine. *(See John 2:3-9)*

Psalms 16:11; "Thou wilt shew me the path of life: in thy presence *is* fulness of joy; at thy right hand *there are* pleasures for evermore."

Various ways of Communications:

In the kingdom of God, which is the government of God; we have various ways of communicating.

Yes, we will be able to talk as we do here on earth using our vocabulary which we speak audibly, but I also believe that our vocabulary will be even greater than ever before once we get to Heaven. The highest level of communicating that I discovered from reading the Word of God and reading after those people who have visited Heaven, is that when they have questions, they will obtain an answer immediately before they have a chance to ask their questions.

Matthew 6:8; "Be not ye therefore like unto them: for your Father knoweth what things ye have need of, before ye ask him."

The reason that we need to ask while here on earth is because it gives God a legal right to move on our behalf (See Amos 3:7, Psalms 115:16)

Again, I believe the primary reason for an audible vocabulary is so we can speak decrees and make declarations of what we want to come to pass.

During Jesus' earthly ministry He taught about the person of the Holy Spirit and His role in the life of believers after His departure from earth and his return to the third Heaven.

You might say what does this have to do with communication in Heaven? As Dr. Roger Mills would say… Jesus said to him, Look, Listen and Learn.

(A) Jesse Duplantis, in his book "Close encounter of the God Kind", said in speaking with Jesus, a thought (questions) would come into his mind and before Jesse could speak it, Jesus would answer him. [5]

(B) Bishop Earthquake Kelley, in his book *"Bound to Lose Destined to Win"* said in his book that He heard a voice say, "You're wondering who those children are." It was clear that this voice was responding to his thoughts. Bishop Kelly was surprised that someone could read his thoughts. He looked around and, although he didn't see anybody, he knew that he was hearing the voice of the Lord. (Dec. 7, 1998 / 2006)

(C) Freddy Vest a Rodeo Cowboy said during an interview on the 700 club that he had a heart attack while sitting on the back of his horse he also remembers having conversations with God. "When he was there, there was communication, but the communication was inside of Freddy and it was nothing that verbally you would have ears to hear or a mouth to speak it."[18]

Jesus taught about the person of the Holy Spirit, and His role in the life of the believers after His departure from earth and return to the third Heaven. In John 14:16-17, 26; 17<u>He dwelleth with you</u>, and <u>shall be in you</u>. 26 <u>He shall teach you all things.</u>

In order to understand the makeup of mankind, there are several scriptures that we need to know that will help us in this area. The makeup of mankind

2 Corinthians 4:16; "<u>outward man</u> & <u>inward man</u>
1 Peter 3:4; "But let it be the <u>hidden man</u> of the heart,
1 Thessalonians 5:23; "Your <u>whole spirit and soul and body</u>

As we examine the Holy Scriptures, we see that Man is a spirit, has a soul that is composed of (Mind, will, Emotion, imaginations), and live in a body
2 Peter 1:13-14; "*this tabernacle (physical house),*

<u>In Colossians 1:13;</u> *at the same time the Kingdom of God come on the inside of our spirit via the Holy Spirit, and He is living within our spirit. (Luke 17:21,* Romans 8:11; 14-16)

   1) The Inward witness – On the inside of each one of us, we have a God tool call sensor mechanism that can be referred to as a *check red-light, stop signal*; it is not a voice that says 'don't do this or that', *It is an inward intuition.*

When you have a velvety-like feeling in your spirit, it is the witness of the Spirit to go the green-light to go ahead signal. Through the Inward witness the Holy Spirit will guide in all the affairs of life, not just spiritual, but natural also, all the affairs of life. The Inward witness is just as supernatural as guidance through vision and so on; it is just not as spectacular. Many people are looking for the spectacular and missing the supernatural that is right there all the time. (*Romans 8:16*)

    2) The Inward Voice *Romans 9:1* "still small voice". The Inward man, who is a spirit man, has a voice – just as the outward man has a voice. We call this voice our conscience. . Your spirit has a voice. Your spirit will speak to you. The still small voice is the voice of our own spirit speaking.

See our spirit picks it up from the Holy Spirit who is in us. Again, that still small voice, that Inward voice, not authoritative, just something on the inside of me that I am going to do such and such. (Elijah, 1 King 19:12)

    3) The Voice of the Holy Spirit *"Acts 10:19-20;"* When the Holy Spirit within you speaks, it is more "Authoritative" – although He is inside you – you look around to see who said it. You think somebody behind you said something. Then you realize it was coming from the inside of you. (*1 Samuel 3:1-19*)

Communications through Visions

Visions: Sometime God leads us through visions. There are three kinds of visions: spiritual vision, trances, and open visions. In a spiritual vision, you see with the eyes of your spirit – not with your physical eyes.

4) Spiritual visions:

Caesarea called Cornelius, a centurion of what was called the Italian Regiment, 2 a devout *man* and one who feared God with all his household, who gave alms generously to the people, and prayed to God always. 3 About the ninth hour of the day he saw clearly in a vision an angel of God coming in and saying to him, "Cornelius!" Acts 10:1-3 (NKJV)

Cornelius was a devout man, but he was not born again. He did not know Jesus because he was a Jewish proselyte. The angel who appeared to him in a vision could not preach the gospel to him. God did not call angels to preach the gospel; however, the angel did tell Cornelius where to send to someone who could preach the gospel to him and tell him how to be saved.

The scripture calls the Cornelius' experience a vision (Acts 10:3). It was a spiritual vision. Cornelius saw in the spirit world, and there are angels out there in the spirit world. If others had been present, they would not have seen anything. Yet if the angel had taken on a visible form, anyone could have seen it. (Hebrews 13:2)

The second type of vision is when a person falls into a trance. Cornelius did not fall into a trance – Peter did.

5) Trance visions:

In Acts 10:9-11; "The next day, as they went on their journey and drew near the city, Peter went up on the housetop to pray, about the sixth hour. 10 Then he became very hungry and wanted to eat; but while they made ready, he fell into a trance 11 and saw heaven opened, and an object like a great sheet bound at the four corners, descending to him and let down to the earth. Acts 10:9-11 (NKJV)

When one falls into a trance, his physical senses are suspended; you do not know where you are at the moment. You are not unconscious, but you do not know what is going on around you, you are more conscious of spiritual things than physical things.

The Third type of visions is called an open vision, your physical senses are intact, your eyes are wide open, and you are aware of what's going on around you, you are not in a trance.

6) Open Vision:

In Acts 8:26-29; "Now an angel of the Lord spoke to Philip, saying, "Arise and go toward the south along the road which goes down from Jerusalem to Gaza." This is desert. 27 So he arose and went. And behold, a man of Ethiopia, a eunuch of great authority under Candace the queen of the Ethiopians, who had charge of all her treasury, and had come to Jerusalem to worship, 28 was returning. And sitting in his chariot, he was reading Isaiah the prophet. 29 Then the Spirit said to Philip, "Go near and overtake this chariot." Acts 8:26-29 (NKJV)

Philip's eyes were wide open, he watched the angel speaking to him, he knew exactly where he was and he knew was going on about him.

See heavenly communications have not changed, as we read about the various means of communication in the Bible, we will see it is the Bible that reveal things about heaven that we should be familiar with.

While here on earth we will communicate via our vocabulary speaking audibly, and as Christians we have the Holy Spirit speaks to us via our spirit, and we have our minds. The mind is the area we have thoughts coming from more than one source, so we can't just accept every thought that drifts into our minds so we must examine them in light of God's Word, and only then are we to receive those thoughts and act upon them.

Again, I believe the primary reason for an audibly vocabulary is so we can speak decrees, and make declarations of what we want to come to pass.

We have the "Inward Witness, the Still small voice of our human spirit, the Authority voice of the Holy Spirit, spiritual vision, Trances, and open vision.

See as a Christian we learn to discern between the two sources of thoughts. We are instructed to cast down the evil thoughts, while receiving the good thoughts of God. *(See Romans 12:1, 2; 2 Corinthians 10:5).*

In Heaven, we can flow in the highest level of communicating by just receiving from God and flowing with Him. Jesse (as mentioned before) in speaking with Jesus, a thought (questions) would come into his mind, and before Jesse could speak it, Jesus would answer him. [5]

Jesus routine: Jesus as the head of His body would not require you to do something that He didn't do. (John 14:12).

Whether we realize it or not we all have a routine, but we are to follow Jesus' routine because He was the sample son. Jesus came to show us how a man being led by the Holy Spirit can walk the face of the earth and demonstrate how to defeat the devil and live in total victory here on earth. If you examine the four gospels, Jesus never called a person to receive him; Jesus did however call for the people to follow Him, meaning to do what He did.

The Apostle of Christ did not get saved until *John 20:22;* "And when he had said this, he breathed on *them*, and saith unto them, Receive ye the Holy Ghost:" This was after Jesus resurrection, and the Apostle they didn't receive the baptism of the Holy Spirit until the day of Pentecost. In *Romans 10:9-10*; we see that you must receive Jesus as your Lord and Savior.

Summary

As we are all familiar with the various acts of brutality that is happening in society, for example the shooting at Columbine High school 15; Virginia Tech, 33; Movie theatre, Aurora, Colorado 12; Elementary school shooting in Newtown, Connecticut 26; Sparks, Nevada 2; Navel Yard in Washington, DC 12; the Westgate mall of Africa 67; and Louisiana church 1.

If we are in tune with the Spirit of God, we would beware of the impending dangerous acts that are about to happen that are being caused by the kingdom of darkness.

In understanding, heavenly Communication, it will help us to be protected from the Cowley act of the devil and his cohorts. Please know whatever you are doing that is not under the direct command of God via the Holy Spirit, verified by the Word of God, is out of the will of God therefore you DO NOT have his guarantee of divine protection, or blessing upon what you are doing.

As we see that the Son of God could do nothing of Himself, what make us suppose that we can do things ourselves separate from the Kingdom of God outside the Leading of the Holy Spirit? If there was ever a time in which we must cooperate with the Holy Spirit it is now. I want to encourage you not to limit this to your personal life; I am talking in ministry, in church services, on your job, and etc.

The essence of this message is that whatever you are about to do as a Christian in co-laboring with God, you must operate in obedience to the voice of God verified by the Word of God. If this is not the case, whatever you doing or about to do, if it is not in obedience to God, it is considered dead works.

"The Holy Spirit is abiding in our spirits and communicates with us through our spirits not through our intellect. Your spirit knows things, you head doesn't know. See we have been taught to listen our heads, and never been taught to listen to our spirits, and we are reluctant to do so.

The understanding that spirit filled believers continually miss, it is because our spirits which should guide us are kept locked away in prison. Knowledge, or intellect, has taken the throne. (Proverbs 20:27) and Proverbs 3:5-6; <u>acknowledge</u> him, and he shall direct thy paths."

Are you being led by the Holy Spirit; or are you being lead by circumstances, situations, and emotions? If you are not being lead by the Holy Spirit you will not know how close we are to the coming of the Lord Jesus Christ. (*See Romans 8:14-16*)

Chapter Three
How to know if you are Operating in the Kingdom of God

In the former chapter we have determined about the Understanding the Kingdom of God is the government of God, and Jesus said the kingdom of God is within you once you are converted. When you are born-again, you have a new spirit, inside our new spirit you have the Holy Spirit, and you have the Kingdom of God within you via the Holy Spirit. Once we make a decision to receive Jesus as our Lord and Saviour, we no longer belong to ourselves, and according to 1 Corinthians 6:19, our body becomes the temple of the Holy Spirit. However, you still have the flesh that is a member that is within our body.

(When a person becomes born-again, they must realize there is the outward body of the man and within its member there something call the flesh that want to do what it has always done and there is the inward man the real you that want to do things that are pleasing to God.)

2 Corinthians 4:16; "For which cause we faint not; but though our outward man perish, yet the inward *man* is renewed day by day."

As Christians, we must become knowledgeable of the Word of God. It is imperative that we become knowledge of "What thus saith the Lord", witness through the knowledge you acquire strength. (See Proverbs 24:5, Hosea 4:6,7).

Once a person has become born-again, there are some things that we need to do before joining any area of the ministry of helps, (Choir, Ushers, Greeters, and etc.) This is a continual process for the rest of your Christians life.

According to Romans 12:1-2; (NLTV) "And so, dear brothers and sisters, I plead with you to give your bodies to God because of all he has done for you. Let them be a living and holy sacrifice—the kind he will find acceptable. This is truly the way to worship him. 2 Don't copy the behavior and customs of this world, but let God transform you into a new person by changing the way you think. Then you will learn to know God's will for you, which is good and pleasing and perfect.

As you can see just from these two scriptures there are some things that as an individual that we must do, see God has done the hard part in giving us a brand new spirit, and we have inside help, the Helper, the Comforter, and the Teacher in the person of the Holy Spirit.

Galatians 5 states and we have listed the works of the Human Spirit, and the works of the flesh. The focus of the Christian's life is followed after the Holy Spirit (within the Human spirit) as He leads you, and not to listen to or give into the flesh. (See Galatians 5:17-25)

The key to maneuvering in the kingdom of God is Peace. Peace comes to us in two forms, both of which will be discussed.

The first type of peace that we are most familiar with, the Peace that the world has to offer which is in the natural. A state of tranquility or quiet a freedom from civil disturbance, a state of security or order within a community provided for by law or custom, freedom from disquieting or oppressive thoughts or emotions, harmony in personal relations.

The world in which we live says to know peace we must either: go some place (Bahamas, Hawaii), buy something (a luxury car which shuts out the harshness of the world), or ingest something (get a prescription for a sedative).

The second type of peace is a Hebrew word SHALOM; which Occur 236 times within the Holy Scriptures, and as you can see listed, it takes 20 words in the natural to define the peace of God. They include completeness, wholeness, peace, health and healing, welfare, safety, salvation, deliverance, soundness, tranquility, prosperity, perfectness, fullness, rest, harmony (unity), the absence of agitation or discord, total well-being (all things intact, nothing missing) In the midst of a stressful life, most people are looking for peace. State of tranquility / quietness, freedom from confusion!

The peace we crave is what Jesus offers is more than that… It is something that Only Jesus can give, Jesus tells us that it is HIS peace that He gives to us. He alone has the authority to extend this peace. It is unique to Him.

Three Stages of Peace

A) *Peace with God* - Because of what Jesus had done - Romans 5:1; "Therefore being justified by faith, we have peace with God through our Lord Jesus Christ:"

B) *The peace of God* - Romans 14:17; "For the kingdom of God is not meat and drink; but righteousness, and peace, and joy in the Holy Ghost." All kingdom expression is love. Colossians 3:15;

C) *The God of Peace* – Is to be manifested from your life Romans 16:20; "And the God of peace shall bruise Satan under your feet shortly. The grace of our Lord Jesus Christ be with you. Amen." The forgiver is within you, Jesus. When you allow Jesus as your forgiver go to that area that is causing frustration. Jesus allows the river of peace.

Who is the Source of true Peace? (John 14:27) This peace is not found in worldly, religious meditation, drugs, and achievements, the peace that we yearn for is something that can only be found in Christ. It may be that the very reason you are here today is because you know that you need something for your life. You know there is an emptiness... you know you need something.

How Do We Get This Peace? (Romans 5:1) Is it really possible to live in continual peace? To the world, that seems like such an impossible goal to achieve. Yet the heart of man yearns to experience peace. Almost continually we hear accounts in the news about different organizations or governments that are trying to bring peace between conflicting groups and nations. Masses all over the world want to live in repose, not excitement.

We can have peace with each other - The peace of the Lord is a peace that restores relationships. All throughout the New Testament we see barriers being lifted between people: Jew, Gentile, black or white, slave, free, male, and female. We all are seeking to glorify Him in our lives. We are not competing with each other we are working with each other. See only through Jesus Christ can we have peace with God, and we can experience the peace of God. (See 2 Thessalonians, James 3:16)

His peace keeps our hearts and minds free of confusion and helps us live victoriously. (See Philippians 4:7-8)

God's name is peace, Jehovah Shalom, The Lord my peace and Wholeness" (Judges 6:24, Matthew 11:28-29, John 14:27), the God of peace, and "the God of Peace shall bruise the satan under your feet" (See Romans 16:20).

The Prince of peace is infinitely more powerful and effective than contending and striving in prayer with an anxious, and troubled spirit, Peace is Power.

Jesus routine: Jesus as the head of His body would not require you to do something that He didn't do. (See John 14:12). Whether we realize it or not we all have a routine, but we are to follow Jesus routine, because He was a sample son. Jesus came to show us how a man being led by the Holy Spirit can walk the face of the earth and demonstrate the devil defeat and live in total victory while here on earth. If you examine the four gospels, Jesus never called a person to receive him, Jesus did call for the people to follow Him, meaning to do what He did.

The Apostle of Christ didn't get save until John 20:22; "And when he had said this, he breathed on them, and saith unto them, Receive ye the Holy Ghost:"

This was after Jesus resurrection, and the Apostle, they didn't receive the baptism of the Holy Spirit until the day of Pentecost. In Romans 10:9-10; we see that you must receive Jesus as your Lord and Savior. See Scriptures References: Mark 1:9-12, Matthew 14:23, Mark 1:35-39, Luke 6:12; John 5:19b; John 8:38; Acts 10:38

1) **Peace of God Governs:** "Today peace ruled in circumstances and with people" Colossians 3:15 – "And let the peace of God rule in your hearts, to the which also ye are called in one body; and be ye thankful."

2) **Peace of God Guides:** "Make all decisions from a place, please." (Colossians 3:15 AMP). Have the peace (soul harmony which comes) from Christ rule (act as umpire continually),

3) **Peace of God Gathers:** "For the saved and the unsaved." Shoes of peace (Ephesians 6:15) "The God of peace shall bruise Satan under your feet" (Romans 16:20) Proclaim peace (Romans 10:15), The bond of peace Ephesians 4:3

4) **Peace of God Guards: "Internal protection and external victory."**– "The peace of God, which passeth all understanding, shall keep your hearts and minds through Christ Jesus." Philippians 4:7. You will keep him in perfect peace, whose mind (imagination) is stayed on you, because he trusts in you. (Isaiah 26:3) The God of peace will crush the enemy beneath your feet. Romans 16:20;

5) **Peace of God Grounds: "It is through practice!"** "For the kingdom of God is righteousness, peace, and joy in the Holy Ghost. Romans 14:17; These things I have spoken unto you, that in me ye might have peace. In the world ye shall have tribulation: but be of good cheer; I have overcome the world. John 16:33; But strong meat belongeth to them that are of full age, even those who by reason of use have their senses exercised to discern both good and evil.

The Enemies of Peace:

There is no peace now for two reasons: the opposition of Satan and the disobedience of man. The fall of the angels and the fall of man established a world without peace. Satan and man are engaged with the God of peace in a battle for sovereignty. (See James 3:16 "giving place to the devil) (See 1 Thessalonians 13:33)

- **Sin** - Rebellion creates strife and distance between our heavenly Father and us. As a result, we feel the conviction of sin, and our peace evaporates.

- **Unbelief** - When we doubt God's promises, uncertainty and fear replace our. Confidence that He will supply all our needs (See Philippians 4:19).

- **Mistreatment** - although criticism from others may threaten our peace, no one can take it unless we give it up. Instead of believing people's unkind or false words, we can choose to hold on to God's peace.

- **Worry** - (Anxiety) is projecting tomorrow's cares upon today results in worry and anxiety, but Jesus said, "Do not worry about tomorrow; for tomorrow will care for itself. Each day has enough trouble of its own" (See Matthew 6:34).

If these were to be banished, we should infallibly enjoy perpetual peace.

Keys to ensure that you walking in Peace:

If you are struggling to find peace, you are not alone. Consider the following scriptural advice to help you find, or regain, that missing peace:

1. **Change your focus**. The Bible instructs us to fix "our eyes on Jesus, who leads us and makes our faith complete" (Hebrews 12:2). As we change our focus -- off of our problems and onto the Lord -- His peace will fill our lives.

2. **Change your circumstances**. Sometimes it is necessary to take a break from the things that trouble us, even for brief periods of time. Even great men and women of God have at times experienced times of devastating discouragement (1 Kings 19:3-5; 2 Corinthians 4:7-10). Try altering your physical setting for a short time. Also, take a close look at your lifestyle. You may be lacking peace simply because you are not following God's pattern for rest.

3. **Change your attitude**. Are you facing a difficult situation? The Bible says, "Whatever happens, keep thanking God because of Jesus Christ. This is what God wants you to do" (1 Thessalonians 5:18). Begin to thank God right now and soon you will experience His peace in the midst of the storm.

Summary

However, Jesus wants to give us peace in every storm, however, in order to have this peace, we must truly understand the gift of peace and have a relationship with the Prince of Peace. If you don't have a relationship with peace, you will have a relationship with the storms of life. Storms will come, but they don't have to overcome you.

Jesus said; "Peace, be still" because He would not allow peace to leave them, once we know the power of peace, no matter what storm or situation satan tries to bring into your life, if he can't rob you of your peace and the storm will not affect you.

The Bible began with peace in the Garden of Eden and closes with peace in eternity. Jesus becomes the peace of all who place their faith in Him. Peace can now reign in the hearts of all those who are His heirs. The peace of Christ is also an unending source of strength in the midst of difficulties.

The work of God begins with peace. Peace is the internal serenity that only God can give. Peace is love in repose, with no borrowing of tomorrow's troubles today. Troubles are not absent. Rather, God is present! When the Holy Spirit is not grieved the dove of peace is able to alight on the heart. Has peace become more and more a way of life for you this year?

The peace of Christ is a great resource in helping us to know the will of God. Colossians 3:15 says, "Let the peace of Christ rule in your hearts, to which indeed you were called in one body; and be thankful." Paul is urging the Colossians to so depend on the peace of Christ that it becomes an umpire in the decisions they have to make in life. Do you have a problem, or a decision to make? Let the peace of Christ make that decision for you.

If you have examined a planned action in the light of God's Word--and His Word does not forbid you from going ahead with it--if you can do it and retain the peace of Christ in your heart, then do it with the confidence it is God's will. But if you find you do not have a sense of peace and God's blessing about it, don't do it. Don't try to rationalize about your decision; you may find it makes good sense from the rational point of view. But will it rob your soul of rest and peace? Do you have a sense of confidence that God is in this? If you don't have peace, it is probably the wrong thing to do. Let Christ's peace be the umpire that makes the calls. That is how we are to govern our behavior.

If you have a personal relationship with Christ, He is your peace and has promised never to leave nor forsake you. If you bring everything to Him in prayer with thanksgiving, His peace will surround and protect you through every situation (Philippians 4:6-7). If you'll simply look to Him, read His Word, and watch Him work in your life, your heart will be calm—even when your circumstances are anything but.

Section II

In this section, we want to establish that every Kingdom has a constitution that the citizens must adhere to if they want to be a lawful citizen within the kingdom and enjoy the privileges and benefits of the kingdom.

Chapter 4
The Constitution

"Study to shew thyself approved unto God, a workman that needeth not to be ashamed, rightly dividing the word of truth" II Timothy 2:15

All scripture is given by inspiration of God, and is profitable for doctrine, for reproof, for correction, for instruction in righteousness:" 2 Timothy 3:16

In every government, there is a constitution, and within the constitution is where the laws, rule and regulations, by which the government operates, or the standard of that government.

The Constitution! The United States is still the symbol of hope for most of the globe. Many people come to the United States after having dreamed of it all their lives. They eventually come here and work hard to create a more respectable life for themselves and for their kinsfolk. At some level, they might be given the chance to join this country (by oath) as a citizen.

When they perform, they cause it to receive and retain all the rights and benefits inherent to citizenship. The trouble is that most don't really understand their benefits, nor really understand their rights. We have many rights and the base document for those rights is our Constitution. Straight off, let's be fair, how many people have read through and understand the Constitution? Not very many.

Not just that, many don't even know where to go to get a transcript of it. You can't read what you can't find.

Likewise, Christianity is a symbol of hope for a dying and decaying world. Many people come to Christ for a better life for themselves and for their family.

They are afforded the opportunity to become a citizen of the Kingdom of God (by oath) and -- praise God -- many do so daily; by repenting of their sins and accepting Jesus Christ as their Lord.

Now, after they are born-again and are citizens of the Kingdom, they, too, have many rights and privileges inherent to this new citizenship.

Our base document is also our Constitution (the Bible). The big difference is that most born-again believers today, unlike the believers in the Old Testament, have free access to our Constitution.

We have copies of it on our coffee table, in our car, on the internet, at church, etc. Now how foolish would it be to become a citizen of a new kingdom and carry around a copy of the Constitution with you all the time and never read it?

Summary:

1. Jesus came to reestablish the Kingdom of God in the earth that was lost by Adam in the Garden of Eden.
2. To show us how to enter into the Kingdom of God and that He was the only door by which one can enter the kingdom of God.
4. His Kingdom has a Constitution that outlines our rights, benefits and laws.
5. Our King has ensured that we have free access to our Constitution.

6. It is our responsibility to read it and clearly understand the rights and privileges to its promises.

7. *II Timothy 2:15* teaches us that as citizens of this new Kingdom, part of our responsibility is to study the Constitution (*2 Timothy 3:16*)

8. Citizens who ignore the Constitution are still citizens, but their ignorance limits them from enjoying the full benefits of their citizenship. Cause you own a copy of our Constitution, the Bible? When was the last time you read it?

CONFESSION

Heavenly Father, I am a born-again believer. I have declared my citizenship in Your Kingdom. I have a copy of the Constitution and I declare that I will read it, study it, apply it, and receive from it. I can have what it says I can have. I can do what it says I can do. I can be what it says I can be. I will never, ever be the same. In Jesus' name, Amen!

Section III

In this section, we listed some of the laws by which we are to apply to our lives if we desire to introduce into the Kingdom of God and enjoy the benefits of being a citizen of the Kingdom of God

Laws establishes the criteria and regulations fixed by the King himself, by which his Kingdom will serve and administered.

The laws of a kingdom are the means by which one ensured or guarantee of the benefits of the King in His Kingdom.

The citizens cannot alter laws in a kingdom, nor are they subject to a citizen referendum or debate. Plainly put, the word of the King is law in His Kingdom. When the laws of the Government of God are violated the blessing stop.

Step Number One
You must be BORN-AGAIN

"Jesus answered and said unto him, Verily, verily, I say unto thee, except a man be **born again**, he cannot see the kingdom of God." **John 3:3;**

Laws establishes the criteria and regulations fixed by the King himself, by which his Kingdom will serve and be administered. The laws of a kingdom are the means by which one is ensured or guarantee of the benefits of the King in His Kingdom. Laws in a kingdom cannot be altered by the citizens, nor are they subject to a citizen referendum or debate. Plainly put, the word of the King is law in His Kingdom. When the laws of the Government of God are violated the blessing stop.

Chapter Five
The Laws of Salvation

Purpose

Man is a sinful creature; therefore, no man is born without sin. However, God demonstrated to us and showed us precisely how much he loves us; in spite of our sins, by giving his only son in order for us to receive everlasting life. The aim of this chapter is to explicate the importance of being reborn. You will learn that being born again is the only way to enter into the Kingdom of God.

God desires us to experience a personal kinship with Him. Although, sin separates us from the relationship that God desires of us, we even have a choice to get a personal kinship with God, by receiving Jesus Christ as our Savior and Lord. We must also repent and ask God to forgive us for our sins.

Upon, reading this chapter, you will also discover the importance of water baptism as well as why we should fellowship in a church. I will explain the initial step that must be taken in order to become a citizen in the Kingdom of God. In order to get the keys to the Kingdom of Heaven, one must be born-again, and on the following pages the purpose and plan of God will be revealed on how to be born-again.

1. **God's Plan – "Now this is eternal life: that they may know you, the only true God, and Jesus Christ, whom you have sent" (John 17:3; NIV).**

   What prevents us from knowing God personally?

   God's Love - "God so loved the world that He gave His only begotten Son, that whoever believes in Him should not perish, but have eternal life" (John 3:16).

2. **Mankind is sinful and separated from God, and then we cannot know Him personally or experience His love.**

   Man is Sinful - "All have sinned and fall short of the glory of God" Man was created to have fellowship with God; but, because of his own stubborn self-will, he chose to go his own independent way and fellowship with God was broken. This self-will, characterized by an attitude of active rebellion or passive indifference, is an evidence of what the Bible calls sin. (Romans 3:23).

   Mankind is separated - "The wages of sin is death" [spiritual separation from God] (Romans 6:23). "... (Those) who do not know God and do not obey the gospel of our Lord Jesus...will be punished with everlasting destruction and shut out from the presence of the Lord..." (2 Thessalonians 1:8-9)

3. **Jesus Christ is God's only provision for man's sin. Through Him alone we can know God personally and experience God's love.**

   He Died in Our Place - "God demonstrates His own love toward us, in that while we were yet sinners, Christ died for us" (Romans 5:8).

He Rose From the Dead - "Christ died for our sins... He was buried... He was raised on the third day according to the Scriptures... He appeared to Peter, then to the twelve. After that He appeared to more than five hundred..."(1 Corinthians 15:1- 6).

He is the Only Way to God - "Jesus said to him, 'I am the way, and the truth, and the life; no one comes to the Father, but through Me'" (John 14:6). It is not enough just to know these truths...

4. **We must individually receive Jesus Christ as Savior and Lord; then we can know God personally and experience His love.**

We Must Receive Christ - "As many as received Him, to them He gave the right to become children of God, even to those who believe in His name" (John 1:12)

We Receive Christ through Faith - "By grace you have been saved through faith; and that not of yourselves, it is the gift of God; not as a result of works that no one should boast" (Ephesians 2:6-9). When We Receive Christ, We Experience a New Birth (Read John 3:3-8.)

We Receive Christ by Personal Invitation

Christ speaking "Behold, I stand at the door and knock; if any one hears My voice and opens the door, I will come in to him" (Revelation 3:20).

Receiving Christ involves turning to God from self (repentance) and trusting Christ to come into our lives to forgive us of our sins and to make us what He wants us to be. Just to agree intellectually that Jesus Christ is the Son of God and that He died on the cross for our sins is not enough.

Nor is it enough to have an emotional experience. We receive Jesus Christ by faith, as an act of our will. You Can Receive Christ Right Now by Faith through Prayer (Prayer is speaking with God) God knows your core and is not as concerned with your words as He is with the attitude of your affection. The following is a suggested prayer:

> **Lord Jesus**, *I want to know you personally. Thank You for dying on the cross for my sins. I open the door of my life and receive you as my savior and Lord. Thank you for forgiving me of my sins and granting me everlasting life. Take control of my life. Make me the kind of person you would have me to be.*

If you pray this prayer right now, Christ will come into your life, as He promised.

How to Know That Christ Is in Your Life

Did you receive Christ into your life? According to His promise in Revelation chapter three and verse twenty, where is Christ right now in relation to you? Christ said that He would come into your life and be your friend so you can know Him personally. Would He mislead you? On what authority do you know that God has answered your prayer? (The trustworthiness of God Himself and His Word)

The Bible Promises Eternal Life to All Who Receive Christ

The witness is this that God has given us eternal life, and this life is in His Son. He who has the Son has the life; he who does not have the Son of God does not have the life. These things I have written to you who believe in the name of the Son of God, in order that you may know that you have eternal life" (1 John 5:11-13).

Thank God often that Christ is in your life and that He will never leave you (Hebrews chapter thirteen and verse five). You can know on the basis of His promise that Christ lives in you and that you have eternal life from the very moment you invite Him in. He will not deceive you. An important reminder... Do Not Depend on Feelings.

The promise of God's Word, the Bible - not our feelings is our authority. The Christian lives by faith (trust) in the trustworthiness of God Himself and His Word. The moment you received Christ by faith, as an act of your will, many things happened, including the following:

1) Christ came into your life (Revelation 3:20 and Colossians 1:27).

2) Your sins were forgiven (Colossians 1:14).

3) You became a child of God (John 1:12).

4) You received eternal life (John 5:24).

5) You began the great adventure for which God created You (John 10:10; 2 Corinthians 5:17; 1 Thessalonians 5:18)

Can you think of anything more wonderful that could happen to you than entering into a personal relationship with Jesus Christ? Would you like to thank God in prayer right now for what He has done for you? By thanking God, you demonstrate your faith.

Suggestions for Christian Growth:

Spiritual growth results from trusting Jesus Christ. "The righteous man shall live by faith" (Galatians 3:11). A life of faith will enable you to trust God increasingly with every detail of your life, and to practice the following:

1. Go to God in prayer daily (John 15:7).

2. Read God's Word daily (Acts 17:11) - begin with the Gospel of John.

3. Obey God moment by moment (John 14:21).

4. Witness for Christ by your life and words (Matthew 4:19; John 15:8).

5. Trust God for every detail of your life (1 Peter 5:7).

6. Holy Spirit - Allow Him to control and empower your daily life and witness (Galatians 5:16-17; Acts 1:8).

The Importance of Water Baptism

The view of most evangelical Christian scholars is that salvation is by grace through faith alone. This is especially indicated by Ephesians 2:8-9; John 3:16; and 1 John 5:1. It is important to understand that baptism is a result of salvation, not a cause.

The professing believer should be totally immersed under water (Greek: "Baptismo" = to immerse). The procedure of immersion is scriptural. The example that we are to follow is found in Matthew 3:15-17.

When we do, we find that there is absolutely nothing we can do as humans to earn salvation. Romans 6:23 tells us that salvation is a "free gift."

We come to Christ through grace by faith, Ephesians 2:8-9 and, our public baptism brings glory and honor to God. Baptism is an act of obedience, and identifying with the death, burial and resurrection of our Lord and Savior Jesus Christ. The motivation to pursue baptism should originate from a desire to show to the world an outward demonstration of the person's decision as well as the inward work the Holy Spirit has already begun in us.

An unsaved person would not likely want to be baptized, because he would not have the Holy Spirit indwelling him to prompt his desire to follow Christ in obedience (unless a sect or cult group has erroneously taught him or her otherwise.)

The fact that one even wants to be baptized (being assured that only faith alone in Jesus Christ saves) is evidence that the Holy Spirit already indwells that person, a result of being born of the Spirit by faith alone.

In the book of Acts, baptism is typically the outward response to coming to faith. It was seen as part of a process which includes:

1) Hearing (or reading about) the gospel,

2) Being convicted and led by the Holy Spirit to confess one's sins (Greek: "Homologeo" means to agree with, to speak the same),

3) Coming to faith in Jesus Christ as Savior,

4) Beginning the progress of growth (which includes repenting from known sin),

5) Joining a group of believers in a local church fellowship,

6) Being baptized. The last two parts are where there are many different opinions among believers and churches.

In order to Yoke Up with Jesus and Kingdom of God Government you must become a citizen of the Kingdom of God. That is done through receiving the Lord Jesus Christ as your own personal Lord and Savior, by doing this you become born again and a citizen of the Kingdom of God. This is step one in Yoking Up with Jesus and Kingdom of God Government.

Fellowship in a Good Church

God's Word admonishes us not to forsake "the assembling of ourselves together..." (*Hebrews chapter ten and verse twenty five*) Several logs burn brightly together; but put one aside on the cold hearth and the fire goes out.

So it is with your relationship with other Christians. If you do not belong to a church, do not wait to be invited. Take the initiative; call the pastor of a nearby church where Christ is honored and His Word is preached. Start this week, and make plans to attend regularly. In order to Yoke Up with Jesus and Kingdom of God Government you must become a citizen of the Kingdom of God and that is done through receiving the Lord Jesus Christ as your own personal Lord and Savior, and by doing this you become born again and a citizen of the Kingdom of God. This is step one in Yoking Up with Jesus and Kingdom of God Government.

Summary

We as humans entered into the world as sinners; but, Glory Be to God, we can all be delivered from our sin right here on earth. We must be born-again and have a personal relationship with God. The only way that is done is to receive Christ into our heart. We receive Christ through Faith and through prayer. Faith believes and prayer is talking to God with a sincere heart.

You can pray this prayer with a sincere heart and Christ will come into your life. Lord Jesus, I want to know You personally. Thank You for dying on the cross for my sins. I open the door of my life and receive You as my Savior and Lord.

Thank You for forgiving me of my sins and giving me eternal life. Take control of the throne of my life. Make me the kind of person you want me to be.".And never leave you alone, and heaven has become your home!

The Bible has four spiritual laws that govern our relationship with God, just like there are physical laws that govern the universe.

The Spiritual Laws are:

1. God's love you and offers a wonderful plan for your life. (John 3:16, John 10:10)

2. Man is sinful and separated from God. Therefore, he cannot know and experience God's love and plan for his life. (Romans 3:23, Romans 6:23)

3. Jesus Christ is God's only provision for man's sin. Through Him you can know and experience God's love and plan for your life. (Romans 5:8, 1 Corinthians 15:3-6, John 14:6)

4. We must individually receive Jesus Christ as Savior and Lord; then we can know and experience God's love and plan for our lives. (John 1:12, Ephesians 2:8,9; John 3:1-8, Revelation 3:20).

Step Number Two
You must be Filled with the Holy Spirit

"And Jesus being full of the Holy Ghost returned from Jordan, and was led by the Spirit into the wilderness," Luke 4:1;

Be filled with the Spirit. Ephesians 5:18;

For as many as are led by the Spirit of God, they are the sons of God. Romans 8:14;

Chapter Six
The Baptism of the Holy Spirit

Purpose

There are three baptisms spoken of in the Bible; this chapter will enlighten you on the baptism of the Holy Spirit and the importance of them. The scriptures of the Bible that come from the book of John states that, the person of the Holy Spirit is the spirit of truth, He is a teacher, He guides us, and He shows us things to come. All things that the Holy Spirit has to offer are needed in order to Yoke up with Jesus and the King of God's Government.

We can receive the Holy Spirit simply by asking. Jesus said, "Ask and you shall receive the Holy Spirit". When the Holy Spirit is invited into your heart, you will be filled with wonder working power. The Holy Spirit is a comforter that we can rely on. The Holy Spirit is a teacher of the truth. Receiving the Baptism of the Holy Spirit is a very necessary step to take in order to Yoke up with Jesus and the Kingdom of God Government.

When we become born-again, the Holy Spirit places us into the body of Christ. This is the first of three baptisms, the baptism of Salvation spoken of in the Bible (Acts 2:38-39). The second baptism is the baptism of the Holy Spirit (See Acts 19:4-12), and Jesus is the one who baptizes with the baptism of the Holy Spirit. The third baptism spoken of in the Bible is the baptism in water (Acts 8:12-14), and this is done by the Pastor within the local church.

In this chapter, I want to share with you my knowledge of the Baptism of the Holy Spirit. The reason that we need the Baptism of the Holy Spirit is because of several key things that He does as the third member of the Godhead. Within the Holy Scriptures, I will list several functions of the person of the Holy Spirit.

According to John 14:17 He is the Spirit of Truth; According to John 14:26 He is the Teacher; According to John 16:13 He is the one that Guides us as believers; and He is the one that gives Revelations according to 1 Corinthians 2:6-12. As we Yoke Up with Jesus and the King of God Government, we need all that the Holy Spirit has to offer.

The Bible simply says, "... be filled with the Spirit" (Ephesians 5:18). You know that the Bible is God speaking to you. The Word of God is the will of God. It is God's will for you to receive the baptism in the Holy Spirit!

In Matthew 7:9-13; says...

> "And I say unto you, Ask, and it shall be given you; seek, and ye shall find; knock, and it shall be opened unto you. ^{10} For every one that asketh receiveth; and he that seeketh findeth; and to him that knocketh it shall be opened. ^{11} If a son shall ask bread of any of you that is a father, will he give him a stone? Or if *he asks for* a fish, will he for a fish give him a serpent? ^{12} Or if he shall ask an egg, will he offer him a scorpion? ^{13} If ye then, being evil, know how to give good gifts unto your children: how much more shall *your* heavenly Father give the Holy Spirit to them that ask him?"

First, we see that you as a son are asking the Father for the Holy Spirit. Even though He has already been given to the Church, you are asking and inviting the Holy Spirit to come upon you and endure you with power.

Ask for the Baptism in the Holy Spirit!

We are told that if we ask, we shall receive. The Word assures us that we will receive the best gift - the Holy Spirit and not a counterfeit.

Therefore, you may ask expectantly and without fear, knowing that your Father gives only good gifts to His children. Jesus said ask and you will receive the Holy Spirit.

In Acts 2:4; says…

> "… And they were all filled with the Holy Ghost, and began to speak with other tongues, as the Spirit gave them utterance".

In Acts 10:44-46; *says…*

> "While Peter yet spake these words, the Holy Ghost fell on all them which heard the word. And they of the circumcision which believed were astonished, as many as came with Peter, because that on the Gentiles also was poured out the gift of the Holy Ghost. For they heard them speak with tongues, and magnify God…"

In Acts 19:6; says "And When Paul had laid his hands upon them, the Holy Ghost came on them; and they spake with tongues, and prophesied".

In these accounts of believers receiving the Holy Spirit and they began to speak with other tongues.

Nowhere in the New Testament does it say the Holy Spirit does the speaking. The believer speaks as the Holy Spirit gives them utterance. You must supply the sound as the Holy Spirit supplies the words. These words will be unknown to you. The Scripture teaches us that in the spirit, we speak mysteries unto God.

In 1 Corinthians 14:2; says…

> "For he that speaketh in an unknown tongue speaketh not unto men, but unto God: for no man understandeth him; howbeit in the spirit he speaketh mysteries.... He that speaketh in an unknown tongue edifieth himself; but he that prophesieth edifieth the church". You are not speaking to man, but to God.

One translation says we speak divine secrets. You can pray beyond your natural knowledge when you pray in other tongues. The Holy Spirit comes to our aid and bears us up in our weakness; for we do not know what prayer to offer nor how to offer it worthily as we ought, but the Holy Spirit Himself goes to meet our supplication and pleads in our behalf with unspeakable yearning and groaning too deep for utterance.

He Who searches the hearts of men knows what is in the mind of God the Father - what His intent is because the Spirit intercedes and pleads [before God] in behalf of the saints according to and in harmony with God's will. (Romans 8:26-27; *the Amplified Bible*)

The Holy Spirit comes to our aid to help us in prayer when we don't know how to pray as we ought and gives us utterance in other tongues, praying the perfect will of God. We need this help. So much of the time we know so little. We may only see a symptom of a much deeper problem.

The Holy Spirit goes right to the root of the problem and prays the perfect will of God for us. In Looking at Jude 1:20; The Amplified Bible: says, "... But you, beloved, build yourselves up [founded] on your most holy faith - make progress, rise like an edifice higher and higher praying in the Holy Spirit." Praying in tongues edifies you.

This means to build up or charge as we charge a battery. I am so grateful to be able to pray in the Holy Spirit. In the Scripture when believers received the Baptism in the Holy Spirit, they spoke with other tongues. This will be a great blessing to you. After you receive your prayer language, pray in the spirit every day. This helps your spirit to be strong and keep rule over your life.

In 1 Corinthians 14:14; says...

> "For if I pray in an unknown tongue, my spirit prayeth, but my understanding is unfruitful."

The Amplified Bible says, "... my spirit [by the Holy Spirit within me] prays...." The Holy Spirit is giving your spirit the prayer or praise. Your voice is giving sound to this spiritual language.

The Amplified Bible says that Cornelius and his household talked in unknown languages and extolled and magnified God. The definition of extol is to praise enthusiastically.

When you receive the indwelling of the Holy Spirit, your spirit will immediately have a desire to express itself in praise to God. How could you help but pour forth praise after having the Holy Spirit, Who proceeds directly from the Father God, come upon you in power?

Your well begins to overflow and rivers are the result! John 4:14, 7:37-39; Spiritual blessings are received by faith - not by sight or by feeling. Your lips may flutter and your tongue feels thick, or you may hear the supernatural words forming down inside your being. Or none of the above may be evident. The lips and tongue are the organs we use to form words.

Your physical instruments of speech - lips, tongues, and vocal cords must cooperate with your spirit in order to give sound to prayer or praise that the Holy Spirit has given. Immediately upon receiving, spiritual language is ready for you to speak. Remember, you have nothing to fear. God has already said that you would receive the real thing. Isaiah 57:19; tells us that God created the fruit of the lips. Do not be concerned with what it sounds like to you.

God will perfect your praise. "... Out of the mouth of babes and sucklings thou hast perfected praise" Matthew 21:16.

"And these signs shall follow them that believe... they shall speak with new tongues" Mark 16:17. Jesus said that the believer would speak with new tongues. You are a believer.

When you pray in tongues, you are praying in the spirit. Just as your native language, such as English, is the voice of your mind, praying in tongues is the voice of your spirit. Therefore, after you ask, speak no more of your native language. You cannot speak two languages at once.

Expect the Holy Spirit to come upon you just as He came upon the believers on the Day of Pentecost, at Samaria, at Cornelius' home and at Ephesus, and you will begin to speak in other tongues as the Spirit gives you the words.

Ask and Receive!

Lord Jesus, I come to You in faith to receive the Baptism in the Holy Ghost. I ask You to fill me to overflowing with the Holy Spirit the same endowment of power that happened on the Day of Pentecost. Cause rivers of living water to flow out of me as I give utterance to my spiritual language. I receive Him now in Your Name.

(Now begin to speak in tongues in praise and adoration as the Spirit gives you words.)

Rely on Your Comforter

Jesus called the Holy Spirit the Comforter, John 14:16. The word used for Comforter means Counselor, Helper, Intercessor, Advocate, Strengthener, Standby. Learn to rely on the Holy Spirit in all these areas of His ministry. He is the Great Enabler!

Jesus said the Holy Spirit is will teach you, not just some things, but ALL the truth. "Ye are of God, little children, and have overcome them: because greater is he that is in you, than he that is in the world" 1 John 4:4. Meditate on this verse and confess it with your lips until your spirit sings with the reality that greater is He that is in you than he that is in the world.

There is one on the inside to guide you who know everything from the beginning to the end. Rely on His guidance and direction in every decision.

Expect His power to aid you in every crisis as well as in everyday life. He is more powerful than the enemy. Satan is no match for Him. This Great One has been instructed to lead you into all the truth. He *will* lead. We are to be quick to follow. He will not only tell you what to do, but will also help you to do it. He will empower you.

The Holy Spirit that created the universe now dwells in you. Allow your mind to grasp what your spirit is telling you. This Great One lives in you! In order to Yoke Up with Jesus and Kingdom of God Government you must become a citizen of the Kingdom of God and that is done through receiving the Lord Jesus Christ as your personal Lord and Savior. By doing this you become born-again and a citizen of the Kingdom of God.

Step one in Yoke Up with Jesus and Kingdom of God Government is being born-again and now you are in a position to take the second step of being filled with of the Holy Spirit or receive the Baptism of the Holy Spirit. Again, the reason we need the Baptism of the Holy Spirit is because of several key things that He does as the third member of the Godhead. Within the Holy Scriptures I will list several of those functions of the person of the Holy Spirit.

He is the Spirit of Truth; He is the *Teacher*; He is one that *Guides* us as believers; and He is the one that gives *Revelations* according and pertaining to the Kingdom of God Government. In our Yoking Up with Jesus and the King of God Government we need all that the Holy Spirit has to offer. (John 14:26; John 16:13)

Receive Strategy from the Holy Spirit

Many times, when speaking about the person of the Holy Spirit, our attention is immediately focused on the person speaking in tongues. The reason for this is because the devil is attacking so many people and trying to sway them from receiving the person of the Holy Spirit and the devil has us in a state of confusion concerning speaking in tongues.

There are many other things that the person of the Holy Spirit has to offer than just the ability to speak in tongues; after all He is the third member of the Godhead. His primary responsibility is to lead, guide, and teach the body of Christ (believers/church) about the things concerning the Kingdom of God.

It is our responsibility is to cooperate (partner) with Him. Remember, the Holy Spirit is the one that empowered Jesus during His earthly ministry. Beginning with the baptism of water, Jesus received the baptism of the Holy Spirit as recorded in John 1:31-34; From this point it was the Holy Spirit who lead and guided Jesus concerning His earthly ministry. The first victory of Jesus was when the Holy Spirit led Him into the wilderness and enabled Jesus to defeat the devil during His time of temptation.

As we examine the book of Acts 10:38; we will find the significance of the person of the Holy Spirit in Jesus life, and He the person of the Holy Spirit desires to be that significant person in our lives if we will cooperate (partner) with Him.

Let's look at several examples in the book of Acts, which is the Acts of the Holy Spirit through the Apostles:

1). We have Phillip, who was a deacon in Acts 6; An Evangelist in Acts 8:29; being instructed by an angel who was sent by the person of the Holy Spirit to join himself to the chariot, to lead the Ethiopian Eunuch to salvation. Then we see the Holy Spirit translating Philip to Azotus.

2). We have the Apostle Peter in Acts 10; the Acts of person of the Holy Spirit through the Apostle Peter in leading Cornelius and his household to salvation. Initially, it began with Cornelius praying and the person of the Holy Spirit sends an angel to Cornelius prayer chamber given him instruction via an angel to send for Peter (Acts 10:7). In Acts 10:20; we see where Apostle Peter has a vision, that was given unto him by the Holy Spirit, instructing "Go with them doubting nothing for I have sent them."

3). We have Acts of the person of the Holy Spirit in the life of the Apostle Paul. In Acts 16:6; we see the Apostle Paul entertaining the idea of going into Galatia; but was forbidden by the person of the Holy Spirit. The Holy Spirit gave Paul a vision in Acts 16:9; revealing that his help was needed in Macedonia, so here we see the Apostle Paul receiving specific direction. As we have seen from these three examples, the person of the Holy Spirit will lead, and guide you. He will give you strategy for what you are supposed to do concerning the Kingdom of God. Remember that He is the third member of the Godhead, He is our helper and we should look to Him for guidance and strategies' concerning every area of our life here on earth and this is not just spiritual things but the natural area as well. (Romans 8:14)

We have many examples of strategies give by the Holy Spirit in the Bible: Let's examine this example in 2 Kings 4:1-7.

What did a certain women do? Now there cried a certain woman of the wives of the sons of the prophets unto Elisha, saying, Thy servant my husband is dead; and thou knowest that thy servant did fear the LORD: and the creditor is come to take unto him my two sons to be bondmen.

1. **What did the man of God do?** And Elisha said unto her, what shall I do for thee? Tell me, what hast thou in the house?

2. **What was the answer given by a certain woman?** Thine handmaid hath not anything in the house, save a pot of oil.

3. **What did the man of God do?** *The Holy Spirit through, the man of God said… Go,* borrow thee vessels abroad of all thy neighbors, *even* empty vessels; borrow not a few. And when thou art come in, thou shalt shut the door upon thee, and upon thy sons, and shalt pour out into all those vessels, and thou shalt set aside that which is full.

4. **What did a certain women do?** So she went from him, and shut the door upon her and upon her sons, who brought *the vessels* to her; and she poured out. And it came to pass, when the vessels were full, that she said unto her son, Bring me yet a vessel. And he said unto her, *there is* not a vessel more. And the oil stayed. Then she came and told the man of God. (Miracle of increase of oil)

5. **What did the Holy Spirit do by His power through, the man of God?** The Holy Spirit said through, the man of God, **Go, sell** the oil, and **PAY THY DEBT**, and **live** (this means that she had more than enough to pay her bills) thou and thy children of the rest. (*2 Kings 4:7 Emphasis added*)

Summary

While Jesus walked the earth, the Holy Spirit was in Him. However, Jesus' physical body was limited to one location, so the effectiveness of the Holy Spirit was limited.

Today, through the body of Christ, the Holy Spirit can saturate the whole earth. When the Holy Spirit came into the earth after Jesus' ascension, He set up residence inside of every believer. Once we are born again, the Comforter lives inside us. We come into the kingdom of God, and at the same time the kingdom of God comes inside of us. As believers, we have the whole kingdom of God inside of us. God's plan is for the kingdom of God to spread throughout the entire earth through the body of Christ.

> John 14:12,16; *"He that believeth on me, the works that I do shall he do also; and greater works than these shall he do; because I go unto my Father. And I will pray the Father, and he shall give you another Comforter, that he may abide with you forever."*

Jesus was saying that we could do the works He did and greater works, or more works, by the Holy Spirit coming to live inside many believers. The Holy Spirit made the whole kingdom available to all who would believe on Jesus. As believers, we now have the kingdom in us, and through us the Holy Spirit will cause the kingdom to manifest on earth as it is in heaven.

In order to be in a position to Yoke up with Jesus and the Kingdom of God Government; one must first be born again and then one must receive the Baptism of the Holy Spirit. The person of the Holy Spirit is available to all of us. Once you are filled with the Holy Spirit, you will find that is all you really need, when the Holy Spirit lives inside of you; He will teach you all that is true, and He will guide you in the right direction. Depend on Him in all aspects of your life; allow Him to instruct you, to lead you, and you can rest assure that you will never be led astray, but give you divine strategies. This is step two in Yoking Up with Jesus and Kingdom of God Government.

Step Number Three
You must walk in (Agape) Love Of God

"A new commandment I give unto you, that ye love one another; as I have loved you, that ye also love one another. ³⁵ By this shall all *men* know that ye are my disciples, if ye have love one to another. " (John 13:34-35)

"This is my commandment, that ye love one another, as I have loved you." John 15:12

If ye fulfil the royal law according to the scripture, Thou shalt love thy neighbor as thyself, ye do well: James 2:8

Chapter Seven
The Royal Law of the Kingdom (Agape) Love

Purpose

There is no love greater than God's love! Love is the law that governs the operation of blessings; therefore, love is the commandment of God. In order to experience God's love for us, we must get to know God and build a relationship with God. Stay faithful and trust God. We are always wanting and needing something from God without really knowing who God is.

Once you learn to walk in love and continue walking in love, you will also have faith, righteousness, healing, prosperity, and gifts of the Holy Spirit. When we walk outside of love, we began to walk into darkness. Darkness is cursed, as believers, we belong in the light. We are born of light because we are born of God, and just as God is light, God is love. Pursue God, build a relationship, and walk in love. Your life will be blessed beyond your imagination.

I believe the message of God's Love is one of the most important massage of the Bible. Many times when a person is a born-again, they try to live the Christian life based upon the love that the world has to offer. In the Kingdom of God, there is a new type of love "Agape" that has been placed in our hearts when we are born again, (Romans 5:5).

I heard this statement and I believe it is true "What you do not understand you will misuse and abuse!"

To walk in THE BLESSING, everything must hang the rod on love. The faith that connects us to it "worketh by love." The fear that disconnects us from it is cast out by love. Walking in love keeps us flowing in THE BLESSING and out of the darkness of the curse. For "He that loveth, abideth in the light, and there is no occasion of stumbling."

I heard a Pastor tell the story of a man who had a vision from the Lord. In the vision, the man was attempting to hang a big and beautiful curtains, but the curtain rod kept falling down. After a few tries, he realized that each of the curtains had meaningful words on them. The words were faith, righteousness, healing, prosperity and gifts of the Holy Spirit.

The man in the vision became frustrated because no matter how hard he tried the curtains would not stay in place. While he worked on one curtain, another curtain would fall. The man finally cried out to the Lord in desperation, and the Lord responded, "Hang the rod!" He looked over and saw a huge golden rod. The rod was big enough to hold all the curtains in place. The rod also had words on it that read, "The Love of God."

I may not have told the story exactly the way that Pastor Winston told it, but the essence is there. In the Kingdom of God, everything hangs on the rod of love or the love of God.

Once you get the rod of love in place along with the curtains of faith, righteousness, healing, prosperity and the gifts of the spirit, everything will hang in place as it should.

Trying to receive the blessings of God without the love of God can be a frustrating experience. Too many people are trying to get things from God without really knowing God at all. Don't pursue things, pursue God. If you pursue God and walk in the love of God, blessings will come to you. Nothing else really works without the love of God operating in your life. Jesus simplified the message of the Bible for us in two commandments: love God and love man. If you can do these two things, then you are giving God, His proper place in your life, and you are, in effect, hanging the rod of love.

Once you have love in place, everything else will stay in place. Love is not just a good idea or a suggestion. Love is THE commandment of God because love is THE law that governs the operation of THE BLESSING.

To fully understand what that means, you must remember that the word law can be defined in two ways. First, there are irrefutable laws such as the laws of nature. Those laws are truth. They cannot be changed, and they always work. The law of physics and mathematics fall into that category. It doesn't matter what form government is in power or what kind of rules men might come up with, irrefutable laws can't be altered. Congress could pass a law declaring two plus two is five, but that wouldn't make it so. The Supreme Court could declare that the law of gravity has been canceled, but it wouldn't matter. Things will still hit the floor when you drop them because gravity always works, and no government on earth can change that.

Although most people think, irrefutable laws apply only to the natural realm. The realm of the spirit is also governed by such laws. The spiritual world is not a place where just anything goes. Its laws are even more exact than natural, physical laws. That's not surprising because God, who is a Spirit, created all earthly matter. He patterned the physical world after the spiritual world.

"Faith cometh by hearing, and hearing by The WORD of God" *Romans 3:27* calls that "the law of faith." It goes into operation when two elements come together a hearer and The WORD of God always produces the same thing: faith.

It doesn't matter who you are, who your parents are, whether you are a man or woman, or what color your skin is, the law of faith works the same way for everyone, all the time. A law that works right alongside the law of faith is found in *Galatians 5:6;* "faith... worketh by love." That is a practical, unalterable truth. There's nothing religious or abstract about it. Faith works by love like a car works by gasoline. No gas, no go. No love, no faith. No faith, no receiving. Like the law of gravity, faith worketh by love is an irrefutable, spiritual law.

The second type of law that exists both in the natural and the spiritual realms is governmental laws. Governmental laws are commands put into effect and enforced by the legal authorities of the land. It is possible to break them, but you will experience the consequences. If you run a red light, you'll get a ticket. Steal a car and you'll go to jail.

God's governmental laws are called commandments. People can and do break them; and when they do, it's called sin. As I've said before, there have been great and absurd debates about what is and is not a sin. But the real definition is simple. Sin is violating the established laws of God.

The devil tries to sell the idea that God established those laws because He is mad at us and doesn't want us to have any fun. But, that's a lie. God gave them to us to keep us from killing ourselves. He put them in place to protect us because He knows, even if we don't, that "the wages of sin is death."

People can argue about it all they want to. They can mock the dangers of sin and say there's nothing wrong with it. But that won't change the consequences. Sin always does just what God said it will do. It sets in motion "the law of sin and death." Sin always leads to death because death is what it produces in the spirit. Adultery, for example, kills. It works death in a family.

There's something that happens in the human spirit, soul and body when a person honors satan by giving him reign in that area. People convince themselves they can contain the damage caused by it. But in reality, opening the door to that one sin gives the devil access to their entire life. He'll take advantage of that access, too. That's just the way he is.

Every fish in the sea and the sea itself all were made by Love's WORD. Love created you. Love breathed life into you. Therefore, everything that is contrary to Love goes against your very substance. Every word of disharmony violates the way you were made. Unloving words, thoughts and actions do violence to the very nerves and cells in your physical body.

(That's why Proverbs 14:13; describe envy as "the rottenness of the bones") No wonder Jesus said that love is the greatest commandment! No wonder He made it a command to love The LORD thy God with all your heart, all your soul, your entire mind and all your strength, and also to love your neighbor as yourself!

When we strive and fuss with others, we become our own worst enemy. We actually begin to self-destruct. When we walk in love, however, we not only BLESS others, we edify ourselves.

In Ephesians 6:8; says, "Whatsoever good thing any man doeth, the same shall he receive of The LORD."

In other words, every act of love, every word of kindness, every loving gesture, enlivens us. The cells in our bodies respond to it. Our minds respond to it. Our spirits expand on the inside of us, strengthening and preparing us to walk in the anointing we were born to carry.

When we take a step outside of love, we step into darkness. That's where the curse is, and it's not where we, as believers, belong. We belong in the light. We are born of light because we are born of God; and just as God is Love, God is Light.'" For ye were sometimes darkness, but now are ye light in The LORD: walk as children of light (*Ephesians 5:8*). The first thing God said at Creation was, "Light be!"

That's why your physical body is electrically operated, and its battery runs on light. Light is the source of our physical power and light is the source of every act of The Royal Law of the Kingdom.

As you have taken Step one in Yoke Up with Jesus and Kingdom of God Government by being born-again. Step two is being filled with of the Holy Spirit or receiving the Baptism of the Holy Spirit.

Now you have been exposed to steps of learning about the highest type of Love, Agape, the love of God that has been shed aboard and poured into your heart by the Holy Spirit; Romans 5:5.

It is very important that you grow and walk in the love of God, because if you fail in this area the other laws will not work because they are all tied to the Royal law of the kingdom which is love. As I mentioned earlier, everything hangs on the Rod of love.

In the English language, we use the one word "love" to express different levels of affection. For example, you might hear someone say, "I love my brother," "I love my mother," I love my wife," "I love candy," I love cars," "I love this," "I love that," and so forth. In each instance, they use the same word: love.

You have to look at the context of what the person is saying to understand the kind of love that they are talking about. The Greek language has four different words that are used to express or define the different kinds of "love."

The first is "**Storge**," which is an affectionate love that exists between parent and child, loyal citizens and rulers, and so forth. The second is "**Eros**," which refers to physical love arising out of passion. The third Greek word for love is "**Phileo**," which is a love that cherishes. An example of this is the love for a brother or a friend. All of these loves – Storge, Eros, and Phileo – should be based on the fourth Greek word for love – "**Agape**,"

The highest kind of love, is God's kind of love, a love that is not based on feeling or performances, but a decision. Agape is a selfless, sacrificial love that goes far beyond anything that most people can even come close to understanding.

When some people are asked to do something for someone else, the first thing they want to know is what I will get in return for doing it. But God's kind of love gives. True love – Agape love does not concern itself with, "What am I going to get out of it?" No, it concerns itself with, "What will this other person gain by my loving them?"

In Ephesians 5:25, Paul tells the husband to love their wives as Christ loved the church. Well, how did Christ love the church? He gave Himself for it, and that's the way we are to love we are to give. In John 3:16, we have a great example of Agape love.

It says, "For God so LOVED the world, that HE GAVE his only begot Son (JESUS), that whosoever believeth in him should not perish, but have everlasting life." God's kind of love will love a person even if that person does not want to be loved.

Agape love, or God's kind of love, even loves a person who doesn't seem to deserve love because of what that person does or says. God's kind of love loves people regardless of their actions. Agape love, it doesn't matter who you are or what you do or what you have done. You can still be loved by the power of God and receive Jesus as your Savior.

Summary

The Royal Law of the Kingdom is love. As God's children, we must grow and walk in the love of God. As humans, we experience different types of love. We experience a love that shows affection between parents and their children, physical love that's filled with passion, a love that cherishes a brother or a friend, and then God's love. There is no greater love! God loves us unconditionally. He loves us even when we don't deserve to be loved. In order to be in a position to Yoke up with Jesus and the Kingdom of God Government we must walk and continue to walk in the love of God.

"This is my commandment, that ye love one another, as I have loved you." John 15:12

If ye fulfil the royal law according to the scripture, Thou shalt love thy neighbor as thyself, ye do well: James 2:8

Step Number Four
Walking Free of Unforgiveness

"²⁵And when ye stand praying, forgive, if ye have ought against any: that your Father also which is in heaven may forgive you your trespasses. ²⁶But if ye do not forgive, neither will your Father which is in heaven forgive your trespasses." Mark 11:25-26;

Chapter Eight
The Law of Forgiveness

Purpose

It is so important that we learn to forgive others; more important than we realize. Holding on to past and present hurt and anger can become destructive. It can destroy our inner-being. Living with an unforgiving spirit can lead to illness; it can keep us from moving forward in a positive light. We also block our own blessings when we choose not to forgive.

This chapter will teach us how to recognize who we need to forgive and the steps we should take to forgive. It will also remind us that in our imperfections we have more than likely wronged someone by saying or doing something and we need to be forgiven as well.

As a child of God and as a citizen of the kingdom of God; we need to understand the Law of Forgiveness. The devil works over night trying to hinder us from being effective for God and His Kingdom.

The devil uses techniques that cause us to operate in unforgiveness. Unforgiveness is a show stopper to keep us from flowing in the promises (power, blessing, anointing and provision) of God.

> Mark 11:25-26; *"25And when ye stand praying, forgive, if ye have ought against any: that your Father also which is in heaven may forgive you your trespasses. 26But if ye do not forgive, neither will your Father which is in heaven forgive your trespasses."*

A lack of forgiveness can block dreams and goals from manifesting in every area of your life. I want to teach you how to recognize and remove them. Sometimes our thoughts, feelings and strategies only need fine tuning for our grandest goals and dreams to come true. Forgiving others is often hard to do because it hurts to extend it to undeserving and hard hearted people.

To release a wrong-doer instead of exacting a just penalty requires that we reach out in love, rejecting the temptation to hold on to bitterness and resentment. This is contrary to our natural inclinations, thus the old adage, to err is human, and to forgive is divine. Forgiveness is not forgetting the wrong that was done; some hurts, cut so deep that forgetting is impossible.

We can forget about the anger and hurt, but the fact remains branded in our minds. Forgiveness takes place when the victim accepts the loss and/or injury done to him and deliberately cancels the debt owed him by the offending person. Forgiveness is an act of your will and God will honor it. But, un-forgiveness, and the resentment and bitterness it generates is deadly. It is optional to forgive or not to forgive, but to be bitter and unforgiving costs far more than it is worth.

Husbands forgive your wives. Wives forgive your husbands. Children forgive your parents.

Anger must be dealt with openly and honestly, not denied or ignored. Either it must be vented in retaliation or the injured party must accept his own anger, bear the burden of it, and confess it in prayer to release himself and to set the other person free.

Revenge always hurts the revenged far more than the one at whom it is leveled! In other words, our pattern must be the grievous and substitutionary death of Christ.

He willingly received the hurt and evil of the entire human race in His own body on the tree (I Peter 2:21-24) to pay the debt for our guilt. He now offers what He has wrought as a free gift to undeserving and guilty persons so they can be free (Romans 6:23; John 10:28-30).

> 1 Peter 2:21-24; *"²¹For even hereunto were ye called: because Christ also suffered for us, leaving us an example, that ye should follow his steps: ²²Who did no sin, neither was guile found in his mouth: ²³Who, when he was reviled, reviled not again; when he suffered, he threatened not; but committed himself to him that judgeth righteously: ²⁴Who his own self bare our sins in his own body on the tree, that we, being dead to sins, should live unto righteousness: by whose stripes ye were healed."*
>
> Romans 6:23; *"²³For the wages of sin is death; but the gift of God is eternal life through Jesus Christ our Lord."*
>
> John 10:28-30; *"²⁸And I give unto them eternal life; and they shall never perish, neither shall any man pluck them out of my hand. ²⁹My Father, which gave them me, is greater than all; and no man is able to pluck them out of my Father's hand. ³⁰I and my Father are one."*

One of the fruits of the Holy Spirit's work in life is the quality of meekness. It is a quality which is nurtured and abetted by practicing forgiveness. This highly prized quality will cause us to be able to accept God's dealings with us as good, without disputing or resisting them.

Meekness will also cause us to be able to bear one another's burdens cheerfully and for Jesus' sake, enabling us to enter into the mystery of Christ's sufferings.

As nothing else will, forgiveness takes us into the mysteries of grace where God forgives us unconditionally on the basis of the substitutionary payment by another

In Mark 11:25-26 says....

> "^{25}And when ye stand praying, forgive, if ye have ought against any: that your Father also which is in heaven may forgive you your trespasses. ^{26}But if ye do not forgive, neither will your Father which is in heaven forgive your trespasses."

Christianity teaches that forgiveness originates with God. Christian believers are taught they are to forgive others as God has forgiven them. God's ultimate forgiveness for the sins or wrongful actions of humanity comes through accepting the blood of Jesus as the ultimate sacrifice and substitute for his justice. They are taught to pray and ask God for forgiveness for their sins. Believer's can gain a release from guilt and fear through the practice of forgiveness. By forgiving others, we learn to forgive ourselves and thus our illusions of being separate can be healed.

Apostle Paul, who played a major role in establishing Christianity said, "Forgive as the Lord forgave you,"

I) <u>WHOM SHOULD I FORGIVE?</u>

You should forgive everyone you can remember, living or deceased, from early childhood right through today. Say an additional forgiveness prayer for anyone you may have forgotten.

You can also forgive institutions, political parties, governments, etc. However, remember that people run these organizations. When all the layers are peeled back, it is still a relationship that we are talking about: It is still a person or persons you are forgiving.

II) <u>HOW DO I KNOW I NEED TO FORGIVE?</u>

You know you need to forgive someone if you feel (or think you might feel) anger, hurt and/or resentment toward them. The first person that popped into your head when you read this is obviously the person you need to begin with, and then proceed in the order that people come to your mind. I can guarantee you that the person with whom you're most angry, resentful and unforgiving will pop into your head immediately.

What if someone needs to forgive me? If you have hurt someone and would like their forgiveness, you can use the forgiveness prayer that I have provided at the end of this chapter. This prayer is the same as the prayer you need to say to forgive others, you're just replacing the words "I" or "Me" with the word "You," or their name. You can still forgive regardless by saying this prayer.

Forgiveness is something you do for yourself, First and foremost, many people have the wrong ideas about forgiveness; they think to forgive means condoning the wrong done against them. They believe they have to contact the people who hurt them and get them involved. They think that forgiveness is something you do for the other people, that it's a selfless act. While all this sounds noble, it's simply not true. Forgiveness doesn't negate bad behavior. Forgiveness doesn't mean you agree with or accept how you were treated. Forgiveness is not to be confused with a pardon.

People should still be held responsible for their behavior, whether it is immoral, unethical, illegal or all three. When you forgive, you are releasing yourself from this person and their actions on all levels. Forgiveness actually places the power back in your hands. Forgiveness also doesn't mean you will allow that person to treat you in a manner you don't deserve again.

Secondly, you certainly do not have to get in touch with the person you're forgiving. Sometimes the people we need to forgive aren't around. They could be in other states, other countries or even deceased. Those you forgive don't necessarily have to know you've forgiven them. The important thing is that you let go and free yourself from the anger and resentment.

Forgiveness breaks break all negativities, although "unforgiveness" isn't an actual word, it should be. We all may have experienced "unforgiveness" at one time or another, by holding back forgiveness, and maybe even nurturing our hurt, anger or resentment. Unforgiveness is a blessing blocker, a show stopper. The negative between you and the personal targets of your unforgiveness actually creates a steel like bond that keeps you tied to them. This negative attachment is stagnant and immobile, and keeps you from being your best self it keeps you from achieving your highest good.

Yes, lack of forgiveness keeps you literally "glued" in a sense to the last person in the world you don't want to be harnessed. It may be difficult to believe that sincerely repeating a simple prayer can free you from your bondage, but it really can free you. It's been proven over and over by talking with true believers.

When you apply the Law of Forgiveness, the negativity that has bonded you to another person, is immediately released, In turn, it releases you to flow in the blessing of God, bringing what you desire, and bringing the highest goodness to you. There are always positive results from forgiving. Sometimes the results seem no less than miraculous.

Breaking negative bonds affects others as well. While the person(s) being forgiven may not know what in the world hit them, they will experience the effects of the negative bond being broken and being released.

The effects on the person that is forgiven are usually positive as well. Their hearts may soften in ways that's unbelievable to them as well as to the people that know them. They may feel the sudden need to call, e-mail or apologize to you seemingly out of nowhere. People who interact with those they have forgiven through this prayer say they are more positive, more pleasant, and even nicer than they have been in years.

Contacting the person you are forgiving is not necessary to contact the other person or persons for the forgiveness to work. For some people, it may not even he appropriate to make contact. You can freely forgive as many people as you choose without leaving your home. It is not necessary to do so in order for the process to work. Usually the person for whom the prayer is being said is quite surprised to hear they are being so freely forgiven.

III) HOW TO ENACT THE LAW OF FORGIVENESS

When I refer to the Forgiveness, Prayer, I am talking about the process described below. You will say this prayer for anyone you wish to forgive, and also to forgive yourself. The prayer of forgiveness that follows will be used for everyone from your childhood to the present. You do not need to reconcile or continue the relationship in order to use the forgiveness prayer. There are three-steps to positively affect difficult relationships. These three-steps will incorporate the Prayer of Forgiveness. In addition, there are two other steps used for relationships, you wish to reconcile, improve or continue.

Make a list is helpful for some of us to make a list of those we would like to forgive. It doesn't matter if it takes you several days or weeks to work through your list.

The important thing is you have begun the process. Make a list of everyone you can think of that you would like to forgive, from your present and from your past. Also, make a list of people you have wronged, whose forgiveness you seek. Forgiveness works freely both ways.

First, set aside a quiet time when you are least likely to be interrupted. Turn off all disruptive electronics inform everyone in your home that you are not to be interrupted. Also, ensure your pets are settled. Sit in a comfortable place and a comfortable position.

Bring the person you wish to forgive into your mind's eye. As much as possible, see them happy and surrounded by love of God. If you have a number of people to forgive, you may wish to complete this in several sessions.

THE FORGIVENESS PRAYER

To bring each person into your mind's eye one at a time, and say:

Heavenly Father, In the Name of Jesus, I forgive each of them _____, _____. Next, visualize then smiling sincerely and accepting your forgiveness. When you say, "and all again is well between us," this means that you are releasing them." It doesn't mean you're now buddies. Next, see that person walking off a stage or out a door, and bring the next person in your mind's eye. You can say the prayer aloud or silently If you are forgiving a group, organization or country, picture the group in your mind's eye and state the forgiveness prayer.

You may even visualize the group members saying the prayer to one another. To make forgiveness real, you must be sincere. It is recommended that you should state the prayer as it is written.

Remember, if you change the words around to continue to justify your anger such as, "I forgive you for not being the person I wanted you to be," or something similar, this means you are not willing to "release" and "let go." Therefore, you will not receive the full benefits of complete forgiveness.

FORGIVE OTHERS

Heavenly Father, In the Name of Jesus, I forgive you completely and freely, I release you and let you go. As far as I'm concerned, the incident that happened between us _____ is finished forever. I wish the best for you. I wish for you your highest good. I hold you in prayer _____. I am free and you are free, and all again is well between us. Peace be with you. Thank You in Jesus name, Amen

Summary

When you really think about the power of forgiveness, no matter what circumstance, situation, or problem you facing; you are the one who is in power as you operate in the law of Forgiveness. Unforgiveness is like being incarcerated for the event that has occurred. See, the devil is seeking for an opportunity to block each one of us from the blessings of God through unforgiveness. When you have unforgiveness in your life, it means that your hands are full, but the moment that you forgive, you are releasing something (someone) and your hands are open to receive the blessing from God. Whatever the devil may bring, we must reorganize so that we are in power, and we can remain in power through the Law of Forgiveness.

Please remember if you don't forgive, the devil wins, but if you forgive, you win. The devil wants to hold you in bondage through unforgiveness, but as you flow in the law of forgiveness you will not to be snared and trapped by the enemy and you will be free to flow in the blessings of God, and enjoy all that He has for you.

Everyone needs to practice the Law of Forgiveness. Even though forgiving others is not always easy to do; it is necessary to do. When we do not forgive someone, but decide to hold on to anger, hurt, and resentment; we are constantly tied to that person. But, being sincere in repeating a simple prayer can release you from that bondage. By engaging in The Law of Forgiveness; you will feel better and unblock your blessings. Also, it is pleasing to God when we learn to forgive and you will be in a position to Yoke up with Jesus and the Kingdom of God Government, we must not allow unforgiveness to operate in our lives.

Step Number Five
Faithfulness, Consistency, Diligence and Excellence

"Blessed are they who maintain justice, who <u>constantly</u> do what is right" (NIV) Psalms 106:3;

Chapter Nine
Faithfulness, Consistency, Diligence and Excellence

In the previous chapters, I have shared a general configuration of the Kingdom of Heaven and basic steps on how to become a Christian/Citizen of the Kingdom of Heaven. In the next few chapters I will share with you the laws and principles by which the Kingdom of God operates. There are four words that I will mention, and they are FAITHFULNESS, CONSISTENCY, DILIGENCE, and EXCELLENCE.

Psalms 106:3 says,
> "Blessed are they who maintain justice, who <u>constantly</u> do what is right" (New International Version).

"A faithful person consistently does what is right, even if it looks like it is not working."

A few years ago I planted a little garden on my back deck, and the first year I received a small crop in return from the seeds/plants that I planted. Peppers, Cucumbers, and tomatoes grew from these seeds/plants that I planted earlier that spring. There were several things that I didn't know the first time I planted a garden. I didn't know the necessity of good black, rich soil, how to keep the bugs and critters (squirrels) out, and the importance of consistently watering the garden. The following year my crop was a much better crop and consisted of: Green peppers, cucumbers, tomatoes, cantaloupes, and watermelons.

First, I got some organic top soil from the local hardware store, I added some horse manure, planted the seeds/plants at the proper time, watered the garden on a consistent bases, and because of these few adjustments along with faithfulness and consistency in doing these things right; I received a greater harvest than the year before.

As I share with you from my application of what I have learned and received from applying natural laws, you will see the same thing is true from our learning of spiritual laws pertaining to the Kingdom of God. In the next few chapters you will learn about the Laws and the principles of the Kingdom of God, but with faithfulness and consistency in applying these laws and principles you will receive what God has promised through His Word. Although we are learning the laws and principles of the Kingdom of God, but it is through Faithfulness and Consistency that maintain our position of Yoking Up with Jesus and Kingdom of God Government.

1. **The Necessity of Faithfulness -** "A faithful person consistently does what is right, even if it looks like it is not working." A few years ago I planted a little garden on my back deck, and the first year I received a small crop in return from the seeds/plants that I planted. Peppers, Cucumbers, and tomatoes grew from these seeds/plants that I planted earlier that spring. There were several things that I didn't know the first time I planted a garden. I didn't know the necessity of good black, rich soil, how to keep the bugs and critters (squirrels) out, and the importance of consistently watering the garden.

The following year my crop was a much better crop and consisted of: Green peppers, cucumbers, tomatoes, cantaloupes, and watermelons.

2. The Necessity of Consistency - First, I got some organic top soil from the local hardware store, I added some horse manure, planted the seeds/plants at the proper time, watered the garden on a consistent bases, and because of these few adjustments along with faithfulness and consistency in doing these things right;

I received a greater harvest than the year before. See each day on a consistence bases I water my garden, because water is a vital part if your garden is to produce what you want.

3. The Necessity of Diligence - Everyone wants to be a success, and most people define success as the attainment of popularity or profit. The most important success, however, is spiritual success, because it brings us closer to God. Spiritual success is found in growing in the grace and knowledge of our Lord Jesus Christ according to 2 Peter 3:18. The way to grow, in part, is found in 2 Peter 1:5-11.

Peter said that we should "give all diligence" or "act with great zeal or effort; to earnestly work" to add these virtues. We must make every effort to muster every ounce we can cultivate these virtues.

Growing strong in Christ does not happen overnight, nor does it happen accidentally or naturally. It requires time, patience and hard work.

Peter also stated in 2 Peter 1:5; and implies in the rest of the verses that we are to "add" each virtue to another. This suggests the idea of each virtue working in harmony with the others to produce an overall effect. They must all be developed in conjunction with each other. We cannot be selective and pick the ones we like and leave others behind.

Many Christians are spiritually immature, and some fall away because they fail to strengthen their faith by adding these virtues to their lives. Some of us may have been devoted children of God for a number of years, but, unless we continue to grow, we are simply repeating the first year over and over again.

4. The Necessity of Excellence - It appears that many have no greater ambition than to be lukewarm, lazy, careless, and undisciplined Christians is not only unbiblical. It is shamefully dishonoring and contradictory to Christ. He gave Himself for us, that He might redeem us from every lawless deed and purify for Himself His own special people zealous for good works.

Mediocrity pleases self or others more than God. Mediocrity grows little in grace and makes little real progress in godliness. Mediocrity prays to satisfy conscience, but not enough to become like Christ. Mediocrity seeks faith without faithfulness, goes through the motions without the master. Mediocrity seeks Jesus as Savior, but not Jesus as Lord. Mediocre faith may fool others; but mediocre faith will not fool God.

What is excellence? Excellence is doing all things well, as Jesus did. In Mark 7:37, we read that the people, after witnessing many miracles and Jesus' lifestyle, concluded that He did all things well. Excellence is a spirit, just as mediocrity is also a spirit. Excellence is a spirit that comes along with accepting Jesus as your Lord and Savior.

Living outside of a relationship with Jesus is mediocrity. Excellence is absolute dependence and trust in God. Caleb said we are well able to take over our inheritance because God is with us (Numbers 13:30/1 John 4:4). The others who doubted God's promises were operating in mediocrity among other things.

God wants His children to take after Him in everything. The spirit of excellence does not drop on anybody's lap. It must be pursued. The bible says, as we behold his face as in a mirror, we are changed from glory to glory (2 Corinthians 3:18). If you will attract excellence, you must stay with God's Word.

It is the Word that imparts unto you the spirit of excellence. According to Romans 12:1- 2, we are instructed to renew or change our mind and not be conformed to this world, but be transformed so that we may prove and attract what is excellent.

Note the words used in this scripture. It says we must not be conformed but be transformed and this is a continuance God wants you to stand out in all that you do. He does not want you to bow or bend to the mediocrity all around you. This world is governed by the devil who is a master of causing mediocre in Christian lives.

According to John 10:10; the scripture says he came to steal kill and to destroy. An excellent mind does not destroy, but puts things right. The believer must stand against everything called average. Excellence is possible if you believe it is possible.

The bible says that nothing is impossible if you are a child of God. You must also operate at this level when believing that nothing God puts in your heart is impossible. In Proverbs 23:7; "says as he thinketh in his heart, so is he." Your thinking will affect your actions, so you must begin to think in excellence. We are to exemplify excellence in all areas of our life, not only in the spiritual, but in our everyday lives, including our marriages, relationships, business and decisions.

The Law of Meditation

"For as he **thinketh in his heart**, so is he:"
Proverbs 23:7;

Chapter Ten
The Law of Meditation

Purpose

The Law of Meditation is living in the Word of God at all times. As children of God, we must learn the importance of meditation. Through meditation we quiet our mind and heart so we can hear God speak to us. When we listen to God and follow his instructions on a daily basis, we are able to live a prosperous and peaceful life. The Law of Meditation shows us that everything we see is in our minds. Whatever we meditate on in our mind determines the way we view what our eyes see. In our mind, we set boundaries, we make unjust decisions, and we tend to stay stuck in situations that have become comfortable to us. Meditation increases the development of the mind. The Word of God provides us with spiritual experience and causes our mind to secure new information and grow spiritually.

In sharing the first four chapters with you, we have focused on laws pertaining to the heart of mankind, and that's where the major changes have taken place thus far. In the next five chapters, I will be sharing laws pertaining to the Soul of mankind with you. In my book "Come and Learn of Me" I write about the makeup of mankind. We are a tripod type being and that means, we are a spirit, we have a soul, and we live in a physical body.

Then I ask the question, "who has your soul"? Within the Soul of mankind are the mind, will and emotions. When a person is saved, their spirit (heart) is changed, but there is still something that has to be done with the soul. Our minds are to be renewed by studying the Holy Bible and downloading what it says about our new life in Christ.

> 3 John 1:2; *"Beloved, I wish above all things that thou mayest prosper and be in health, even as thy soul prospereth."*

When we live in the Word *of* God, our soul prospers, and our lives are filled with joy and satisfaction. Our minds are renewed with God's Word, and we walk in the truth. As an apostle of the church, John said he had no greater joy than to hear that those under his leadership were walking in truth. That has got to be the heart's cry of every pastor and church leader, and it certainly is mine. I want to see every member of every church, and everyone who hears the teaching and preaching of God's Word, walk in truth as a result of ministry.

God's truth has many facets, but when it comes to living successfully and happily on planet Earth, we must live within the safety and provision of His laws. God's laws, both natural and spiritual, is the absolute truths by which His Kingdom functions.

Therefore, we should know His laws and live our lives according to them if we want to live productively and peacefully. Many people have come to understand God's natural laws and work with them. Whether or not they are saved, they have been able to develop and invent wonderful things just by discovering God's laws.

For example, mankind has taken the laws of aerodynamics to cause airplanes to fly. They developed the television, the internet, and other forms of communication and entertainment in the field of electronics. The discovery of electricity and the laws governing it have revolutionized our lives.

Human beings have accomplished all of these things and still the world is in turmoil. Why? Only knowing Jesus Christ can change the very inward nature of a person from being sinful to righteous. As believers, we take this one step further. Only when Christians live by God's spiritual laws can their outward life reflect their new, godly nature and impact the world around them.

The way Joshua and the children of Israel were going to possess the Promised Land by meditating on God's Word day and night. (Joshua 1:8)

Today we must possess the promises of God by operating in this same law. We are to literally live in the Word of God at all times. Jesus taught us the Law of Meditation. (See John 15:7)

Then said Jesus to those Jews which believed on him, if ye continue in my word, then are ye my disciples indeed; and ye shall know the truth, and the truth shall make you free (John 8:31-32)

Jesus is the Living Word, and when we abide in Him, we abide in the Word of God. He and the Word are the same.

Jesus is Truth, and meditating in the Word day and night is how we know the truth, and how we are set free, forever. This is also how we get our prayers answered. How this works, again, is very simple.

When we think the way God think and pray according to His will and Word, then we will have whatever we pray. The catch is we must believe what we are praying. Our physical eyes are the gates through which we contact the world around us, but our minds determine what we actually see with them. How our minds think and the knowledge and wisdom contained in our minds determine what we actually perceive. The Law of Meditation shows us that everything we see is in our minds. What we meditate on is going to determine the way we view everything our physical eyes observe.

When the twelve spies went into Canaan, only two of them saw a great land given by God and prepared for them by God. What they saw in their minds gave them the inspiration and ability to possess it. Why? They were meditating on God's Word, and His promises, day and night.

They were seeing what God saw and thinking God's thoughts; therefore, they were able to do what God said to do. The other ten spies still had their eyes on themselves, thinking about what they wanted and what they were capable of doing. They were not meditating on God's promise, so they saw only giants and a land too great to possess. This is a perfect example of how a renewed mind can make the difference between success and failure, just as God told Joshua. The enemy knows how God's laws work, so he perverts them to accomplish his own evil purposes.

In 2 Corinthians 4:4; the Bible says that the devil has blinded the minds of those who do not believe God's Word. Notice, it did not say he blinded their eyes.

It said he blinded their minds. We don't see with our eyes; we see through them. We actually take pictures with our minds. The mind is the lens that gives focus to the picture we are taking. Our perspective is formed in our minds.

Meditation deals with the internal, subconscious mind. The subconscious is like a gauge. It holds down growth and expansion—it holds back redevelopment. It doesn't want you to stop doing what you are used to doing. Your subconscious sets the boundaries—makes decisions whether you want it to or not without your conscious participation. The landmarks it sets prevent you from going either below or above a certain level, it will reject any change to keep you in the comfort zone.

God designed us with a subconscious mind that is on automatic pilot to keep us alive and functioning automatically. However, meditation changes all that. It provides you with a spiritual experience that causes your subconscious to look into new information. The Word of God will provide you with a spiritual experience and cause your mind to lock into new information.

Caleb had a different outlook or revelation from the other ten spies, which enabled him to say, "Let us go up at once and take possession, for we are well able to overcome it" (see Numbers 13:30).

Jacob received new information through a dream from God. The dream not only delivered him from years of servitude and financial bondage to Laban, but also caused a transfer of great wealth to come into his hands. (See Genesis 31:10-12.)

The subconscious is affected by repetition and pondering the Word—by reading it slowly, hearing the Word, often in quiet and rest until your subconscious receives new information. It has the power to transform you. The devil and his demons try to plant all kinds of ungodly images and thoughts in the minds of people so that when they see the truth they will not recognize it or receive it. We must always remember that the devil and his demons have no truth in them.

Ye are of your father the devil, and the lusts of your father ye will do. He was a murderer from the beginning, and abode not in the truth, because there is no truth in him. When he speaketh a lie, he speaketh of his own: for he is a liar, and the father of it. (See John 8:44)

If our minds are renewed in God's Word, we will take a godly picture and see as God sees. If our minds are not renewed, or if we reject His Word, we can be deceived and blinded by the devil to see what he wants us to see and the devil is a liar and the father of lies. If we do not keep our minds renewed and continually submit our lives to the Word of God, the enemy can lead us down the path of destruction and even death.

The Way to living the Christian life

One of the things the devil will do is try to complicate everything. But, everything God does is easy enough for a child to understand and accomplish. Take the law of gravity. It is very simple. Everything is pulled to the Earth's surface because the Earth is spinning on its axis.

Children understand very easily that if they are standing on a chair and jump off of it, they will go down to the ground. They will not fly up into the air.

They don't need to know the full scientific explanation to accept the truth and live by it, but it is available to them.

This is why Jesus said that we must become like children to be born again and live the Christian life.

> Matthew 18:3-4; *"Verily I say unto you, except ye be converted, and become as little children, ye shall not enter into the kingdom of heaven. Whosoever therefore shall humble himself as this little child, the same is greatest in the kingdom of heaven."*

Little children believe what their parents tell them, and they are totally dependent on their parents for love, provision, and protection. That is the way we are to be with almighty God our Heavenly Father.

We are to believe everything He tells us in His Word and rely completely on Him for everything. Life becomes incredibly simple when we do this, and we understand that everything He asks us to do is simple. Whether it is sowing seeds of faith, abiding in His Word, feeding and clothing the poor, forgiving those who hurt us and offend us, or seeking first the Kingdom—all of His commands are simple. God's laws are not only simple, but they are also consistent.

When I say consistent, I mean they work the same way every time, and they will work for everyone. If it is a law, it will work the same for you as it will for me. The law of gravity will work whether you are poor or rich, white or black, male or female, old or young. The Law of Meditation is no exception. It is simple. Anyone can do it. And it will work the same for everyone. That is why the devil will take this law and deceive people with it. He knows it will bring results. So he gets people meditating on things other than God's Word.

Meditation that the devil inspires can bring a season of pleasure and even temporary good into their lives, but ultimately they will find themselves in greater bondage than when they started because they are not meditating on God's Word. They are meditating on things that are not of God.

In recent years the church has stayed away from meditation because there have been so many cults based on some type of meditation. The Occults and the New Age Movement in all its forms offers numerous ways of meditation, from Transcendental Meditation, Yoga Meditation and Silva Mind Control.

Some minds are blinded by the enemy to meditate on what he wants them to meditate on. He deceives them in their minds. They believe they are doing something good, but they are following the greatest liar in the universe. We must remember that the enemy has never had an original thought. The devil has never created anything.

The Bible says that all things were created by and for Jesus Christ (see Colossians 1:16). The devil and his demons can take only what Jesus created and pervert it for their purposes.

So the enemy has come up with a multitude of ways to get us to meditate on anything but God's Word. That is how he can keep our minds blinded, keep us from believing, and keep us under his control. Unfortunately, the church has seen all these eastern religions and cults become popular in recent years and many believers have decided that meditation is of the devil.

They forgot that God gave the Law of Meditation and that it is a key to our ability to possess all that Jesus died to give us everything from peace within to financial prosperity without. Therefore, we must look at what the Bible has to say about meditation and practice it as God instructs us.

What is Biblical Meditation?

The Bible was originally written almost entirely in Hebrew and Greek language. A particular word may be translated in one English translation and meditate in another translation, or with similar words such as ponder, consider, imagine or muse.

The point is, in the Bible, meditation is never portrayed as a religious, mental or emotional ritual. It simply is directed thinking, reflection, contemplation or concentration.

Certainly the quality of our thinking can continue to improve, especially when we regularly pray for God's guidance. Prayer, Bible study and meditation take time. God wants us to think and speak His Word over and over; pondering it in our hearts like a cow chews its cud. If you are a city-person, let me explain this analogy.

A cow will chew grass and swallow it, which is like the first time you hear the Word and receive it. Then, the cow will regurgitate what it has just swallowed and chew it some more. This release more nutrients. Likewise, when you continue to muse on Scripture, to speak it out, ponder it, mutter it, and ask the Holy Spirit about it, you are going to continue to get more and more revelation from it. The cow continues to do this until all the nutrients in the grass are ingested into its system.

This is where meditating the Word differs; because there is no end to the revelation we can glean from God and His Word! Again, it is so simple! We meditate on His Word day and night and we become one with the Living Word. The Word literally transforms us and enables us to be like Jesus and do the works of Jesus. As long as we are meditating on God's Word, we will do well. And we must always keep in mind that if God's Word is not transforming us, then whatever else we are meditating on is transforming us.

The law of Meditation will transform Your Life because it is the most powerful yet simple key to living a joyful and successful Christian life. The simpler the truth, the greater its power, this is God's design. Human being, with the help of the devil complicates life and messes it up! Understanding and practicing the Law of Meditation gives you a confidence that says, "This situation is a real challenge, but I know that if I just meditate in the Word and see this problem the way God sees it, then I will know the truth and be free. I will have His wisdom and be able to make a decision to follow the path that is His will. A special note about meditation will cause you to override sense knowledge.

Summary

The Law of Meditation is good for the soul! Meditating on God's Holy word will help us and keep us moving in the right direction. Reading the Word and meditating on the Word consistently transforms us and enables us to be as Jesus wants us to be, because it's through meditation that the Word of God will become a part of us.

Also, it is through meditation we will receive a revelation from God. As we continue through meditation we can receive new revelation from the Holy Spirit, and this will keep us in position to Yoke Up with Jesus and Kingdom of God Government. You may be surprised of how many Christians are allowing themselves to be pulled out of position because of an old revelation.

The Law of Faith

Where is boasting then? It is excluded, by what law? of works? Nay: but by the **law of faith**. Romans 3:27;

Chapter Eleven
Law of Faith

Purpose

The law of faith is safe and dependable. Faith is the law of God and it pleases God when we abide by that law. Faith is based upon the word of God and not what can be seen with the human eye. Operating in the law of faith requires us to know the word of God, a heart that believes in God's word, and a mouth that speaks God's word.

According to the Webster's dictionary, the meaning of the word law is, a principle based on the predictable consequences of an act, condition, etc.

Example of other laws:

The law of Faith is like God's law of gravity. It works. Believe it or not, it still works. The law of gravity works all the time. God's law of faith works all the time, as it's God's Law of Attraction! Electricity has laws, and there are also laws of aerodynamics. If you operate within the laws of electricity or aerodynamics, it is safe, performs well and is dependable. However, if you break these laws, they can kill you.

Likewise, if you operate within the law of faith, it, too, will be safe, it will perform for you, and it will be something to depend on. The problem is that some people don't "work it." The law of gravity is mandatory. The law of faith is optional. But God tells us how to operate in faith. It will work whenever it is applied properly. Faith will not work if we fail to apply it according to God's specified way.

Faith is a law in the sense that electricity has laws, and there are also laws of aerodynamics. If you operate within the laws of electricity or aerodynamics, it is safe, performs well and is dependable. However, if you break those laws, it can kill you. Likewise, if you operate within the law of faith, it, too, will be safe, perform for you, and will be something to depend on.

In Romans 3:23-27;

> "For all have sinned, and come short of the glory of God, 24: Being justified freely by His grace through the redemption that is in Christ Jesus: 25: Whom God hath set forth to be a propitiation through faith in His blood, to declare His righteousness for the remission of sins that are past, through the forbearance of God 26: To declare I say, at this time His righteousness: that he might be just, and the justifier of him which believeth in Jesus, 27: Where is boasting then? It is excluded, by what law? of works? Nay: but by the **law of faith**.

All of Believers have a measure of the God kind of faith

For I say, through the grace given unto me, to every man that is among you, not to think of himself more highly than he ought to think; but to think soberly, according as God hath dealt to every man the measure of faith. (See Romans 12:3) Mankind has a free will to place it in, and exercise it on, whatever he wants.

In fact, man is a creature of faith. That is to say that he was created to live by faith. Man is driven by something in him to place his faith, (like an anchor), in something or someone with the desire to feel safe, sound and whole.

It really becomes a matter of just what his faith is in, as to what result will come of it. For example, his faith may be in his education, his money, his strength, his doctor, his lawyer, his preacher, and on and on.

Faith is the Law of God

> "Faith is the substance of things hoped for and the evidence of things not seen" (Hebrew 11:1)

We please God when we operate in Faith.

> "But without faith it is impossible to please Him: for that who comes to God must believe that He is, and that He is a rewarder of those who them that diligently seek him." (Hebrew 11:6)

We believe that the carnal mind cannot operate in GOD'S LAW OF FAITH.

> "Where is boasting then? It is excluded, by what law? of works? Nay: but by the law of faith." There are other laws like this, for instance, the law of the Spirit of life and the law of sin and death" (Romans 3:27)

> "There is therefore now no condemnation to them which are in Christ Jesus, who walk not after the flesh, but after the Spirit, For the law of the Spirit of life in Christ Jesus hath made me free from the law of sin and death." (Romans 8:1-2)

> "For l say, through the grace given unto me, to every man that is among you, not to think of himself more highly than he ought to think; but to think soberly, according as God hath dealt to every man the measure of faith." (Romans 12:3)

> "If any of you lack wisdom, let him ask of God, that giveth to all men liberally, and upbraideth not; and it shall be given him. ⁶ But let him ask in faith, nothing wavering. For he that wavereth is like a wave of the sea driven with the wind and tossed. ⁷ For let not that man think that he shall receive any thing of the Lord."
>
> (James 1:5-7)

It also states in James that we have to be doers of the Word of God.... not just hearers. We have to put our faith to work. Speak it, believe it without doubt!

We find the following in the book of James says...

> ²³ For if any be a hearer of the word, and not a doer, he is like unto a man beholding his natural face in a glass: ²⁴ For he beholdeth himself, and goeth his way, and straightway forgetteth what manner of man he was.
>
> (James 1:23-24)

Faith Obeys the Word! - You have heard the adage "seeing is believing" well, that's not really true. The Bible indicates that "Believing is seeing through the eyes of Faith."
(2 Corinthians 4:18).

True Faith is never blind. Faith always knows. Faith always sees. Faith is able to look through the storm and see the end results. Faith will always talk the end results, instead of what exists at present. Faith is acting on the Word of God!

The key to Understanding the Workings of Faith

Mark 11:22-24; "But shall BELIEVE that those things which he SAYS shall come to pass; he shall have whatsoever, (Anything in line with the Word of God), he SAYS In verse twenty four;" therefore I say unto you, what things so-ever ye desire, when ye pray, believe that ye receive them, (Prior to their manifestation), and ye shall have them. (Emphasis added)"

You have to SPEAK His Words concerning healing. **You are SPEAKING them too:**

> 1. Confess (affirm) to God
> 2. Proclaim to the devil and
> 3. Confirm to yourself that you BELIEVE what you are saying.

In James 2:17; The Word of God tells us, "Even so faith, if it hath not works, is dead, being alone."

You must ACT on your faith for it to be released and produce anything! The withered hand had to be stretched out before it was made whole.

In Matthew 12:9-13; the Word of God says…

> "⁹And when he was departed thence, he went into their synagogue: ¹⁰And, behold, there was a man which had his hand withered. And they asked him, saying, Is it lawful to heal on the Sabbath days? That they might accuse him, ¹¹And he said unto them, What man shall there be among you, that shall have one sheep, and if it falls into a pit on the Sabbath day, will he not lay hold on it, and lift it out?

> ¹²How much then is a man better than a sheep? Wherefore it is lawful to do well on the Sabbath days. ¹³Then saith he to the man, Stretch forth thine hand. And he stretched it forth; and it was restored whole, like as the other."

We need to DO something that we could not previously do. Our faith has to be based on the written Word of God, whether it is for healing or anything else!

Faith, the Operation of God

Faith is acting on the WORD. It is not on your sensory mechanism, some philosophical reasoning, nor on theological concepts, but it's acting on God's Word.

> "If you confess with your mouth that Jesus is Lord and believe in your heart that God raised him from the dead, you will be saved. For it is by believing in your heart that you are made right with God, and it is by confessing with your mouth that you are saved.
> (Romans 10:9-10 NTL)

> "²⁷Where is boasting then? It is excluded By what law? Of works? Nay: but by the law of faith."
> (Romans 3:27)

In order to participate in the operation of faith you must have three things:

1. You must have the Word of God (Logos\Rhema)
2. A Heart that believes the Word of God (1 Peter 3:4)
3. A Mouth that speaks (confesses) the Word of God
(Proverb 18:21)

Some scriptures are given to show what the Word of God is teaching us the secret of faith is to be a co-labor with the Spirit of God, it is necessary to know what the ground rules are so that we can operate in faith.

Listed below some examples of the Operations of Faith:
1. God said, "Let there be" Genesis 1:3-25;
2. Abraham "Father of many nations" Genesis 17:3-40
3. Conquest of Jericho: Joshua 6:16 -20;
4. Naaman, the Syria healed: 2 King 5:1-4, 8-14;
5. Peter is acting on the Word of God. Luke 5:1-9;

The simplest way to the operation of faith is to learn to believe the Word and act on it. You don't know if you are really a believer until you are willing to demonstrate your belief. It is through acting on the Word of God that you move from believing to faith. James chapter one and verse twenty two; states that, "We are not to be hearers only, but doers of the Word of God."

The operation of faith calls those things, which be not as though they were. Instead of them being based upon what you see; they are based upon the Word of God. The universe, in which live, contains many laws. Again, everyone is very familiar with is the law of gravity. Everyone knows what goes up must come down.

The law, by which we access the things of God, is called the Law of Faith. The Law of Faith operates when we learn to "Call those things which be not as though they were", (2 Corinthians 4:18).

We can apply this law, because we are born-again.

"We have the same spirit of faith, according as it is written, I believed, and therefore have I spoken; we also believe, and therefore speak" (2 Corinthians 4:13)

There are many who operate in faith from a negative prospective. Listed below are some examples of negative phrases that people use without realizing it.

1. "My feet are killing me." (1 Peter 2:24)
2. "I am scared to death." (2 Timothy 1:7)
3. "I am confused." (1 Corinthians 14:30)
4. "I am broke, busted, and can't be trusted" (Phil. 4:19)
5. "Well, if it's not one thing it is another" (Mark 11:23)
6. "I am so weak" (Joel 3:10b)
7. "Girl I am about to lose my mind" (1Corinthians. 2:16)

We, as believers, have the ability of operating in faith without an understanding the workings of faith. It is the enemy who is influencing us to use such phrases because he knows that it is detrimental to our lives. By understanding the proper working of faith, we can receive the wonderful blessings of God.

"Therefore being justified by faith, we have peace with God through Our Lord Jesus Christ: By whom also we have access by faith into this grace wherein we stand, and rejoice in hope of the glory of God and not only so, but we glory in tribulations also: knowing that tribulation worketh patience;" (Romans 5:1-3)

As believers, we have the God kind of faith and must act according to Mark 11:22-24;

> "²²And Jesus answering saith unto them, Have faith in God. ²³For verily I say unto you, That whosoever shall say unto this mountain, Be thou removed, and be thou cast into the sea; and shall not doubt in his heart, but shall believe that those things which he saith shall come to pass; he shall have whatsoever he saith. ²⁴Therefore I say unto you, what things soever ye desire, when ye pray, believe that ye receive them, and ye shall have them."

I trust that you have seen from the biblical examples how the operations of the God kind of faith, works. In order to be successful in the things of God, it is necessary to know what the ground rules are, so that we can be co-laborers with the Spirit of God. It is through faith that we have access to the wonderful blessings that He has for us to enjoy while on earth.

Example: In my life, I remember a time when I was preparing to attend Bible College. I was living in New Jersey and the school I was planning to attend was in Tulsa, Oklahoma. April of 1981, I made a list of what I needed in order to attend school in Oklahoma.

The list is as follows:

1. I had a car that I needed to be transported to Oklahoma.
2. I needed a truck to take my personal belongings.
3. I had a house that needed to be rented.
4. I had a family that I needed to relocate.
5. I needed a job to support my family.
6. I needed a house for my family.
7. I needed some money.

Once I completed my list of what was needed in order to move to Oklahoma in April of 1981, I PRAYED THE PRAY OF FAITH for everything that I needed on that list. I lived near a park that was about a mile in length and each day after work, I walked around that park giving thanks to God that I believe that I receive everything on my list, and counted it as done by Faith. I did this every day until I left at the end of August of 1981, (approximately one hundred and forty days). Around the second week in August my friend, Timothy, who was already in Tulsa, Oklahoma, was coming to New Jersey for a wedding. I was able to contact him, and he was able to drive my car back to Tulsa Oklahoma. Number 1, getting the car transported to Oklahoma was removed from my list.

I received my last paycheck at the end of August. After paying my last few bills I had only $300.00 left. Therefore, I had enough money to rent a Ryder truck. I gathered up my family (wife and two sons).

Number 2, needing a truck to load and carry personal belongings was removed from my list.

I remember saying to God, "If I end up in Timbuktu, it is on you, because I believe that I am doing what you want me to do." Remember, I still had my list of things that I believed that I receive everything on my list, and I had counted it as done by faith.

In the natural, our house had not been rented and we did not know where we were going to stay once we got to Oklahoma. I did not have a job lined up, and I only had a $300.00 in my pocket.

I remember heading south. Just before we got on the New Jersey Turnpike, I call my pastor, Clinton Utterrback, of Redeeming Love Christian Center, to tell him that we were on our way. Just in case you don't understand, I believe I heard from God, and I took Him at His word with no backup plan.

As we traveled to Oklahoma, and stopped to fill up the Ryder truck, it costs $50.00 each time. I remember I was down to my last $50.00 somewhere in Pennsylvania. After filling up the truck, I went in and paid for the gas. When I got to the truck, and started to get back in, I saw an envelope. I picked it up and got into the truck.

I looked in the envelope and it contained all one hundred dollar bills ($2,500.00). As cool as I am, I stayed focused and continued on my way to Oklahoma. As we continued on our way, I was just praising God for the financial blessing. I was thinking that somewhere along the line, somebody would give me some money. After all, I was a Christian, I had a lot of Christian friends, and they knew I was relocating my family to Oklahoma so I could attend school. I thought, maybe the church, or some of my friends would give me something, but no one did. Number 7, needing money, was removed from my list!

What I did was act upon the Words that God had given me, and for the first time, I saw firsthand that God watched over His word and performed it in my life. As I checked my list, I checked off numbers 1, 2, and 7. My house still had not been rented, I still did not have a job, nor did I know where my family and I were going to stay.

Once we got to Oklahoma we checked into a hotel, and within that first week, I met a fellow student by the name of Kevin. Kevin and his family lived in a large house that had a studio apartment with a kitchen, fireplace, and 1 1/2 bathroom. My family and I moved in and lived there for a while. Number 4, relocating my family was removed from my list! Eventually, we got the whole house, and were able to rent out the studio apartment. Number 6, needing a house for my family was removed from my list!

Within that same week, I got a job at the PepsiCo Bottling Company as a computer operator. I worked there the entire time that I was in Oklahoma and continued to work there even after finishing school. Number 5, needing a job to support the family was removed from my list!

By the end of September, our house in New Jersey had been rented. The same tenants lived in our house the entire time we were in Oklahoma. Number 3, renting our house was removed from my list! I want you to know that God is faithful to His word, and as a child of God all we have to do is take Him at His word and act on it. The Word of God works if you work it.

Summary

Faith is trusting in God and not man. For man has the ability to fail, whereas, God never fails. When you walk by faith, there is no room for doubts. When you walk by faith, there is no time for worries. When you walk by faith, mountains will be moved. Always know God's word, have a believing heart and confess with your mouth God's word. According to Hebrews 11:6, it states that without faith it is impossible to please God, but as we Yoke up with Jesus and the Kingdom and the Law of faith we will always be in faith, thus always pleasing our Heavenly Father.

The Law of Tithing

"Woe to you, scribes and Pharisees, hypocrites! For you pay tithe of mint and anise and cummin, and have neglected the weightier matters of the law: justice and mercy and faith. **These you ought to have done, without leaving the others undone.**

(Matthew 23:23)

Chapter Twelve
The Law of Tithing

Purpose

In this chapter, you will learn what tithing is, the importance of tithing, and why we should tithe. The portion that God requires of us to tithe is only ten percent. First and foremost, tithing is being obedient to God and secondary it is reveling what's in our hearts.

The principle of Divine Ownership means that God is the owner of everything. Understanding the Principle of Divine Ownership helps Christians to realize the problems they may have when it comes to giving and tithing. Tithing is 'Holy' unto God. Therefore, out of our one hundred percent, ten percent for the Lord should be set apart and given to the Lord first.

Tithing is a law that was established by God in the Garden of Eden. The law of tithing is found in the book of Genesis (Book of Beginnings) and continues throughout the Bible. Tithing is a means by which God tests our obedience, tithing is putting God first, and demonstrating where our heart is.

Also, tithing is a means of how His work here on earth is to be maintained or financed.

What is Tithing?

Tithing is returning ten percent of the one hundred percent of what God had blessed you with. The first portion of the 100 percent is what God has entrusted you with when you are obedient, and the ninety percent is redeemed and blessed. The tithe is simply the basic starting point in our Christian financial commitment.

The definition of tithe is derived from the Hebrew word, ASAIR, which means to give the tenth part of according to STRONG'S EXHAUSTIVE CONCORDANCE.

God has given mankind the exclusive right or dominion to rule over His property and world. We have not only been given the right of dominion, but we are also "free moral agents," able to make our own decisions and to determine our own actions. Therefore, man can bless God with his actions or curse God with his actions. Obedience blesses God, while disobedience is a reproach unto God. Tithing brings blessings, while not tithing obviously brings a reproach. You are cursed when the devil is able to rob you of what you have. It is obvious when you are not being blessed because God made a promise to rebuke the devil, and if you are not blessed, then you must be cursed.

Divine Ownership

If this principle was understood in the hearts of all Christians, then the problems associated with giving and tithing would be over. Therefore, I will quote several scriptures to support this principle. Please take the time to read each scripture. In fact, underline them in your own Bible for future references.

I have listed several scriptures showing that God owns everything, and it has been His decision to allow us to share in part of His creation. (See Psalm 24:1, 50:10-11, Haggai 2:8, Ezekiel 18:4, 1 Corinthians 6:20, 10:26).

See God owns everything and we are merely stewards over His possessions! Based upon the above scriptures and many, many others, it is clear that the entire earth, world, gold, silver, animals, and all people are God's!

The principle of divine ownership teaches us that there is **NOTHING** that does not belong to God! Whereas, the principle of dominion teaches us that mankind has been given stewardship over God's property. Not only the tithe, but everything else: 100% belongs to Him. We are simply stewards being obedient to our Heavenly Master Jesus Christ, our LORD and Savior.

Law of Tithing

1. **Garden of Eden:** Genesis 2:15-17; And the LORD God took the man, and put him into the Garden of Eden to dress it and to keep it. And the LORD God commanded the man, saying, of every tree of the garden thou mayest freely eat: But the tree of knowledge, of good and evil, thou shalt not eat of it: for in the day that thou eatest thereof thou shalt surely die.

Notice that in giving Adam and Eve stewardship of the Garden, God gave them every tree from which they could eat freely except for one. Exercising faithful stewardship of the Garden meant leaving that one tree alone.

They were not to take that fruit for themselves and consume it. Being faithful stewards meant life to Adam and Eve. By choosing to eat the fruit of the tree, they were acting like owners rather than stewards.

Isn't that precisely how the principle of the tithe operates for us? God gives us stewardship responsibility over our lives. Even though it all belongs to Him, He richly gives us all things to enjoy (see 1 Tim. 6:17). But He has asked us not to touch the first fruits. "The tithe and the first fruits are mine," says the Lord."

When we demonstrate faithful stewardship, we show God that we realize we are stewards, not owners. We also demonstrate faithful stewardship when we tithe.

1. **ABRAHAM, AND MELCHIZEDEK: (See Genesis 14:18-20, Hebrews 7:1-10)**

A full 430 years before tithing was a part of the Mosaic Law; Abraham tithed to Melchizedek. According to the book of Galatians, Abraham is our spiritual father and Melchizedek is a type of Jesus Christ (some prominent Bible teacher's think he might even have been Jesus Christ Himself!). Melchizedek's titles were "king of righteousness" and "king of peace"- and, of course, Jesus is the true King of righteousness and peace.

We also know that Melchizedek is a type of Christ because the Bible explicitly says so. In Hebrews 5, the inspired writer says of Jesus: (See Hebrews 5:9-10)

The seventh chapter of Hebrews is devoted to showing how Jesus is the fulfillment of all the types and shadows embodied in Melchizedek. It gives particular attention to the fact that Abraham tithed to Melchizedek. (See Hebrews 1-3)

So Abraham, our spiritual father, tithed to Melchizedek, who was either Jesus Christ Himself or a symbolic representation of Christ. Moreover, all this occurred 430 years before the Law.

2. **PATRIARCH JACOB: GENESIS 28:22;** "And this stone, which I have set *for* a pillar, shall be God's house: and of all that thou shalt give me I will surely give the tenth unto thee.

In Genesis 28, we find the patriarch Jacob has his famous encounter with God in a dream, with a rock as his pillow. His life and heart, having been changed, he rises and says: (See Genesis 28:22)

Jacob's vow to tithe came straight from his grateful heart. That's what I want you to see. True tithing comes from the heart not from a legalistic mind. I also want you to note that this promise came 400 years before the Law.

Like his grandfather Abraham, Jacob wanted to give God the first of his First fruits, the first 10 percent. Having experienced the sweetness of God's presence and the goodness of His favor, Jacob wanted to bless Him.

> 3. **MOSES UNDER THE LAW (COVENANT):** 'We see another insight into the power of tithing in Leviticus 27. We find God giving instructions to the Israelites about how to prosper in the land of promise: (See Leviticus 27:30)

God considers the tithe holy. The word "holy" means "separated" and "set apart." In other words, the first 10 percent is to be separated and set apart for the Lord. It is not for me to determine what to do with it. It is God's tithe. (See Deuteronomy 26:1-2, 13-14)

When you understand that the tithe is holy, you don't want it in your house. You want to get it to the house of God where it belongs. You don't use part of it for your vacation. You don't use it to pay for your children's school tuition. You know that holy means set apart. As we have seen through the timeline of the Old Testament, please note that God is a God that changes not! **God said "I change not"** (See Malachi 3:6)

4. Jesus said *"these ought ye to have done,"* and not to leave the other undone.

The New Testament isn't silent about the law of the tithe either. In fact, Jesus made a very plain statement on the subject. (See Matthew 23:23)

Jesus is obviously scolding the Pharisees here. He points out that they are meticulous about tithing, but that they have neglected the weightier matters of the law. There is one other important point mentioned later in this passage that I want you to see. (See Hebrews 7:8)

According to this remarkable verse, Jesus receives tithes in heaven. When you write your tithe check, you may think you're giving it to your local church, but in a very real, spiritual sense, true tithers have their offerings received by the Lord Jesus Himself who present ministry is our High Priest. What a privilege! What a holy thing?! What a loss for those who never take the step of faith and tithe.

We are talking about the tithe as the base of God's relationship with man. The tithe is the Lord's and I'd like to establish some facts about the tithe. Not only are you commanded to tithe, but you are charged by God to see that the church functions faithfully in this matter. The promise of God is that the windows of heaven will be open for those that will walk in this truth.

Tithing isn't really giving — it's returning. It is bringing back to the Lord what is already His. Thus, the principle of multiplication is that finances over and above the tithe must be shared if they are to multiply. Also that it says Tithes and Offering.

In Matthew 25:21; Jesus tells a story of three stewards. One steward was entrusted with five talents. When accounting time came around, he returned those five talents, to the Lord, plus five more. And the Lord said, "Well done, good and faithful servant".

God wants your finances to be blessed, and He wants your finances to be multiplied. But it is vital to understand that you will never see the multiplication of your finances until you understand these two principles:

> 1. We give to the Lord first so that our finances are blessed. The Tithe is to be brought into the local church. This is the means by which God takes for His house. God promises to pour us out a blessing that we will not have enough room to receive.

> 2. What we give over and above our tithes is an offering because only that which is shared can be multiplied. The principles of multiplication are as powerful today as they were during the Old Testament and the beginning of the New Testament times.

Tithing is God's way of supporting His work. In your relationship with God, and to show your love for God, you will bring that which is His to Him. God will faithfully reward you for your love to Him.

The Law of tithing was before the Mosaic Law, It was practiced during the time of the Law, and it is to continue during the dispensation of GRACE. It belongs to God, it is holy, and it must be brought to the church. He will bless you if you will pay your tithes, and curse you if you don't.

In the context of operating kingdom principles, you must tithe. If you fail to tithe, the principles will not work. The object of this book is to share with you the various laws within the kingdom of God and how they operate. Align yourself with the laws and enjoy the blessings of the kingdom of God. In order to flow in the Blessings of God and have manifestations of Supernatural Provision we must be in alignment with the law of tithing.

An Illustration to help understand the reason for Tithing!

To give a practical illustration from scriptures in the book of Exodus, Levities, and Numbers we see there were the Twelve Tribes of Israel were: Benjamin, Ephraim, Manasseh, Naptali, Dan, Asher, Issachar, Judah, Zebulon, Simeon, Reuben, and Gad. The Levites were a tribe of High Priests who were chosen to render service at the tabernacle; while in the wilderness, each tribe was camped strategically around the Tabernacle of God. Eleven out of twelve was to bring the tithe a tenth to the Lord. Aaron and the Levities were priest unto the Lord, and they were not to be involved in the ordinary cares of life, the other tribes of Israel's were to bring a the tithes, to take the House of God, and the House of God and The priests and his family would be taken care of the Tabernacle. (See Ezekiel 44:30; Haggai 1:5-9)

These scriptures give the indication that if the House of God and the man or women of God is not taking care of through tithing. The man or women of God is not free to bless you or your house. As we come to the modern times, we have the Church building (the church is the people of God, born-again believers) the church building is where believers meet to worship, receive instruction by the Holy Spirit via the man or women of God, to receive conformation of things reveal to them.

The church building is supposed to be the lighthouse of the community; but many times the neglect houses in the community are taken care of better than the House of God.

Executive members of the Body of Christ (Apostles, Prophets, Evangelists, Pastors and teachers) **are to neglect neither physical needs nor ministry of the word.**

Jesus gave Apostles; and some, Prophets; and some, Evangelists; and some, Pastors and Teachers; For the perfecting of the saints, for the work of the ministry, for the edifying of the body of Christ: Till we all come in the unity of the faith, and of the knowledge of the Son of God, unto a perfect man, unto the measure of the stature of the fulness of Christ (See Ephesians 4:11-13, Acts 6:1-7)

Again, we come to the modern times, we have the Church building (the church is a living organism of born-again believers) the church building is where believers, the living organism come to worship. The church building is supposed to be the lighthouse of the community, be supported by the tithes of the believers; but many times church organism (born-again believers) is more a concern of their house, or home that they neglect the houses of God in the community, and are taken care of better than the House of God.

Ten benefits (Rewards) of tithing:

I have also included Scripture references for you to check out.

1. **God is pleased with your obedience.** Regular giving is a sign of obedience to Christ. We prove our love for Christ by obeying his commands. (See Malachi 3:10; Isaiah 1:19)

2. **God is honored by your faithfulness.** Proverbs 3:9 He deserves our faithfulness. (See Proverbs 3:9-10)

3. **Tithing helps to keep your priorities straight.** Matthew 6:21 I believe that giving to the Lord is the number one priority for a believer. (See Matthew 6:21)

4. **You are eligible for a blessing.** The blessing is not always monetary, but very could be a business opportunity, and invention, to write a book, and etc. God has blessed with a Covenant that promises "health and wealth" to the Christian that part of Salvation provision that must be claimed and beyond we as believers have an Inheritance. (See Malachi 3:10)

5. **Guards Christians from selfishness.** Tithing reminds us that ultimately our money does not belong to us. (See Acts 20:35)

6. **God loves a cheerful giver.** Are you excited about the opportunity to serve God with your finances? (See 2 Corinthians 9:6-12)

7. **Tithing supports the Great Commission.** Your tithe should go to your local church and God has chosen to work through the church during this age. (See Matthew 28:19,20)

8. **Tithing ensures that your needs will be met.** God has promised that our needs will be met. Needs – but not necessarily "wants". (See Matthew 6:33)

9. **Tithing helps to meet the needs of God's people.** Hopefully your church seeks to use at least a portion of its budget to help those less fortunate. (See 1 Corinthians 16:1,2)

10. **Tithing reminds us that God is the true owner and giver of all that we have.** All that we have belongs to God and the tithe helps to remind us of this fact. (1Timothy 6:17,18)

I believe that tithing is a commandment, although it is not listed with the Ten Commandments does not dismiss the significance of it or make it a suggestion, We have 613 biblical laws that were given, but we see that Abraham pays tithes before the Laws was given. The reality is that the tithe is just the *beginning* of your obedience to Christ.

I have been asked many questions like what about giving my tithes to help a family that has in trouble rather than given my tithes to my local church? Or can I give my tithes to a charitable organization like the Red Cross? No! The tithes are specifically to be given to the local church, again this is how God finance the work of His kingdom. Please note this that you don't know why some people are in the predicament that they are in, and if you help them in their mess, you can cause their mess to come to your house.

After you have paid your tithes, then you are to give and offering or sow your seeds and then you can be blessed, because then and only then can you be blessed, because you know at the point where God has something to work with. If you are trying to sow seed and reap a harvest it's not gone to work because without PAYING your tithes you are robbing God.

Given to the local charitable organization; I don't because God has raised up local ministry organizations and as the Holy Spirit leads I give to them. Jesus said the world will take care of itself. Look at how many millions were given by the world for the victims of the World Trade Center bombing, Boston is bombing victims, and etc. I am not saying that you shouldn't give to charity, but I give to a Ministries Organization that God has set up for that purpose. The tithes are for a specific purpose and that is the local church.

Is there a Penalty for not tithing? (See Malachi 3:8-12)

I have a question? Do you think an unrepented thief or a robber will be allowed to enter Heaven? Statistics stated that only 12% of the Body of Christ are tithers, what do you think will happen to the 88% of non-tithers?

Summary

"What hast thou that thou didst not receive?"
(See 1 Corinthians 4:7)

God gives us so much! And, out of all that he gives and blesses us with, He only asks us for us to tithe (Tenth) back to Him a measly ten percent. Tithing shows our love and obedience to the Lord. Tithing is also Kingdom Laws and Principles. Trust and believe that when you tithe, God will pour you out a blessing that you will not have room enough to receive. See, it is through the law of tithing that we Yoke up with Jesus and the Kingdom of God Government, and receive that blessing that He promised. This is the means by which Kingdom work is financed in the here now earth, and He will bless with even more. If you are not a tither put God to the test!

The biblical references which address the tithing issues are: Genesis 14:20; 28:22; Leviticus 27:30-32; Numbers 18:20-28; Deuteronomy 12:6,11,17; 14:22,23,28; 26:12; 2 Chronicles 31:5,6,12; Amos 4:4; Malachi 3:8-10; Matthew 23:23; Luke 11:42; 18:12; Hebrews 7:5-9.

The Law of Sowing and Reaping

While the earth remaineth, seed-time and harvest, and cold and heat, and summer and winter, and day and night shall not cease. Genesis 8:22; 1 Corinthians 9:6-12;

Chapter Thirteen
The Law of Sowing and Reaping

Purpose

In this chapter, I want to help you understand the principle of sowing a seed and reaping and receive a harvest. In order to understand the principle of seed-time and harvest, you need to know the purpose of the seed, the process of the seed, the power of the seed, and the sowing and planting of the seed. Even if you don't have a seed, God will provide you with a seed. The seed must be planted where God wants it planted. The seed will be blessed and produce a harvest that is good and plentiful.

Within the Word of God, there is a principle of seed-time and harvest *(Genesis 8:22)* everything began with a seed. You and I as human beings, all started out as a seed *(Genesis 1:9-12)*. So regardless of who you are, God can take whatever you have as a seed. I remember hearing the story of a particular young man in a particular service.

When the offering was taken during the service and the plate was passed to him, the only thing that he had to give was a pencil. God honored his act of faith and today he is a well known minister of the gospel and has a TV broadcast that is seen around the world.

Let's look at an example from the Old Testament. (2 Kings 4: 1-7). Elisha asks her, "What shall I do for you? Tell me, what do you have in the house?" God is always more interested in what we have than what we don't have. The widow was telling Elisha what she didn't have, but he wanted to know what she did have. What she didn't have could not help her or anybody else. But what she did have was the seed to her miracle.

The oil she had was small in amount, and she was asked to place it into large vessels. She could have been excused for thinking that the little she had was insignificant. But sown in obedience to the prophet it was multiplied and became a blessing to her and to others. Even in a time of need, taking a financial seed and sowing it in good soil is our way into the provision of God.

The Kingdom of Heaven is built on the generosity and giving, because the answer to the need is always in the seed. Never think your seed is too small to sow into a large ministry. Trees grow from mustard seeds and great oaks were once an acorn! Keep sowing!

If you don't have a seed, God has promised to give you a seed *(2 Corinthians 9:10)*. Most Christians never take time to study this principle. As I examine the above verse of scripture, I see it as a win win situation for me. Why? Because God has promised to give me the seed and all that He asks of me is that I plant it in the ground as He instructs. He will multiply the seed that He told me to sow, and that's not all!

He will cause that seed to produce a harvest large enough for me to have something to eat (minister bread for my food), and enough that I can plan again (increase the fruits of my righteousness). I don't know about you, but I think that's a pretty good deal all I have to do is to obey Him.

We need to understand the principle of seed-time and harvest. "… We must recognize 1) the purpose of the seed, 2) the process of the seed, 3) the power of the seed and finally, 4) the sowing and planting of the seed."

In sharing with you God's plan for financing the gospel of the Kingdom of Heaven, this principle is very significant in the economic system of God. There must be a seed-time if you are going to have a harvest. Most people want a harvest time without a seed-time. (Acts 20:35)

The world has a saying: "get all you can, and sit on all you get." In the economics system of Heaven, it is just the opposite (Luke 6:38).

1. The Purpose of the Seed - The seed is to produce a harvest, so that you can fulfill God's assignment, but most of us are in such a financial mess that we need help first. When we give, our giving will produce receiving; our receiving will increase to the next level.

Let me explain what I mean. For example, when being led by the Holy Spirit you give $100; that $100 is not leaving you. Using the principle of seed-time and harvest time it just became your employee. It will begin to work for you as a servant to make money for you and bring it back to you.

2. Your Seed is Powerful - God is revealing to us divine Principle, because He wants us blessed. Sometimes if we are not careful we underestimate the potential of a seed. An example of this can be found in Genesis 26:1-5.

3. The Power of the Seed - Never underestimate the potential of a seed. In Genesis 26:12; Isaac received a hundredfold return. According to the Word of God, we never know what a seed can produce, but one thing I do know is that you cannot beat God by your giving (Luke 6:38).

There is no limit to what God can do. This is a spiritual law and it will produce supernatural results. Spiritual laws cause us to tap into another realm, another dimension (2 Corinthians 9:10; Ecclesiastes 11:1-3).

4. The Process of The Seed The word "sow" means to plant seed for growth by scattering or to scatter (as seed) upon the earth for growth.

First - Remember is to always give God your best seed. In order to do that; you must listen to the Holy Spirit and obey Him. Sometimes the best seed may put a strain on you, but that is okay.

Secondly - The sower's heart must be in the sowing. For example, when offering time comes around, do not just pluck a few bills in the bucket with the rest of the congregation because it is the right thing to do. No!

The sower must know what he or she is doing. Sowers have expectations of a harvest. Every time you plant, you make a demand on that seed. Therefore, you make a demand on the harvest. Do not turn it loose, and do not let the devil send you a seed and call it a harvest. When it is a harvest, you will not be able to carry the harvest in the same container in which you carried the seed.

Thirdly - Understand the soil. As you are sowing to God the best seed, check out the soil. The seed and the soil never limit God. It is always the devil or the sower who limits God.

Whenever and whatever you sow a seed into make sure you plant your seed in good soil. Do your research. Most ministries or churches have websites, and most Evangelistic type ministries have websites, and there should be data concerning the amount of money that come in each year and how it is being used.

Also, there is a website that has various ministries and these sites have investigated different ministries to see if they are doing as they say.

Finals - (Ecclesiastes 11:4) will help you understand this principle. What is the meaning of 'he that observeth the wind'? "It means if you are waiting for everything to get right before you start sowing – the economy, the stock market, your job, your boss giving you a raise – you will not sow. You must sow by faith, even though it looks like your company is about to shut down. If God told you to sow that seed, sow it, because He is trying to get you out of the financial mess you are in."

The objective is that as you go through the process of sowing a seed and reaping a harvest:

1) You break free of the world system, which is most important.
2) You should become a tither on a regular basis.
3) You should be in a position where you will have more than enough to meet your needs and also be able to help finance the gospel of the Kingdom of Heaven.

Again Tithing isn't really giving – it's returning. It is bringing back to the Lord what is already His. Thus, the principle of Seed time Harvest, the Law of Sowing and Reaping can only work when we give over and above our tithes is an offering or SEEDS and only that which we give beyond the Tithes can be multiplied.

This was God's intent from the very beginning. But we; His children, do not realize how caught up we are in the world's system. Thank God that He has provided a way for us to break free. Just keep on Sowing and Reaping

Sowing and Reaping is the principle by which you break free of the world system. The average job is designed to pay you enough to come back on Monday. The mistake that most Christians make is that they are trying to live off their paycheck, but your job is designed as just one place where you can get some seeds. After paying your tithes, and offering, start practicing the principle of Sowing and Reaping and know that God can bless you with a harvest that can be more than your paycheck.

The objective of this book is to share the various laws within the kingdom of God and how they operate. We must make the adjustment to come into alignment with the various laws and enjoy the blessings of the kingdom of God through Yoking up with Jesus and Kingdom of God governments.

In order to flow in the Blessing of God and have manifestations of Supernatural Provision we must be in alignment with the principle of Sowing and Reaping.

Summary

Trust and believe in God with all your heart. God is rich in houses and land and he wants to bless us with riches. Do not allow the devil to place fear into your spirit and make you afraid to sow a seed. Stop living from paycheck to paycheck, which is the system of the world, and start practicing the principles of sowing and reaping. Trust that God can and will bless you with a bountiful harvest. When we practice the law of sowing and reaping we are Yoking up with Jesus and the Kingdom of God Government.

The Law of Favor

"For thou, LORD, wilt bless the righteous; with favor wilt thou compass him as *with* a shield." Psalms 5:12

Chapter Fourteen
Law of Favor

Again, as we have said before the Laws of the Kingdom are the proclaimed words, decrees, and edicts of the king. These laws determine the standards by which the kingdom is to be governed. "The law of Favor is the sovereign prerogative of the king to extend a personal law to a citizen. These are the positions that citizens are giving to receive special privileges and advantages that are personally protected by the king"

> "And he said, I will make all my goodness pass before thee, and I will proclaim the name of the LORD before thee; and will be gracious to whom I will be gracious, and will shew mercy on whom I will shew mercy." (Exodus 33:19)

What Is Favor?

Just as with any law, in the law of God's favor, you will still find boundaries, but the fences are a little further off than what you are most likely used to. There is a freedom to roam and you can explore and practice more in life when walking in God's favor because your favor-walk with God is about learning, not doing.

It is about experiencing Him in the moment and this cannot be done with things that are based on the law but rather based on faith. Consequently, to walk in favor we need to stop, look and listen to the voice of God and only the voice of God. We need to be more obligated to the approval of the Father than we are committed to the flattery and pleasing of men. We need to obey rather than sacrifice (or serve if you prefer, 1 Samuel 15:22).

Following God is a choice that requires us to do things that are sometimes unpopular or unexplainable, but is always for the benefit of the kingdom and not necessarily to the benefit of others. Sometimes this will cause a conflict to arise when your call diverts you from the call of others who expect you to join yourself to them. But you should not be swayed away from what God is doing in you if He has called you do to something. He is big enough to handle the issues in the kingdom. What he needs is people who will humble themselves, pray (2 Chronicles 7:14), and for us to speak the truth in love no matter how difficult it is.

If there is one thing about God's law, it is absolute. Good or bad, God's laws are black and white and the fact is, most of us are more comfortable and feel safer when we can see the boundaries that contain us.

This is the way the law works. It is a bit like prison walls that do not let prisoners get so much of a glimpse of the outside world. It is all about isolation and protection - the world from you and you from the world. The opposite is true of walking in God's **favor**. Walking in the favor of God requires faith and a trust relationship in knowing that God will not reject you even in your missteps.

Most of us do not believe we deserve God's favor. And yet, like any dad who wants to bless his kids, God is no different. He loves to show His children favor (1 Samuel 2:26).

Favor means to endorse. Say for instance, someone has written a book and wants someone to endorse it, someone who has established themselves to endorse their book; hopefully this will help them sell more copies of their book, Favor means to give support, it may be a tangible way of encouraging someone or to assist them.

Example of Angels can assist, also showing God's endorsement of what you are doing.

> "Bless the LORD, ye his angels, that excel in strength, that do his commandments, hearkening unto the voice of his word." Psalms 103:20

> "Are they not all ministering spirits, sent forth to minister for them who shall be heirs of salvation? (Hebrews 1:14)

Angels come to assist as we go forth doing the will of God;

> "Behold, I send an Angel before thee, to keep thee in the way, and to bring thee into the place which I have prepared. ₂₁Beware of him, and obey his voice, provoke him not; for he will not pardon your transgressions: for my name *is* in him. ₂₂ But if thou shalt indeed obey his voice, and do all that I speak; then I will be an enemy unto thine enemies, and an adversary unto thine adversaries. ₂₃ For mine Angel shall go before thee, and bring thee in unto the Amorites, and the Hittites, and the Perizzites, and the Canaanites, the Hivites, and the Jebusites: and I will cut them off." (Exodus 23:20-23)

See as citizens of the kingdom of God, we need some assistance as we go forth in the Lord. The assistance can be human or divine 'angels' (See Hebrews 1:14). Favor is an anointing over your life that will make things easier. This anointing will take the struggle out of everything and gives us a sweat less victory.

Favor means to provide with an advantage, give us insight that will put us ahead of the game. Favor means to show special privilege, or to showcase someone, or to prove someone, or to pick someone out, or to feature you or someone.

Allow me to share this with you, these are some of the ideas of what Favor is, so that you can picture in your mind what the favor is.

See Favor is part of your heritage or inheritance, when you examine the scriptures you will see favor is something that God gives us to cause us to be successful, where we normally would fail, or cause a door to be open that would normally be closed. See there are some things that favor will cause to happen in your life. It starts when you are born-again, and we must be taught about favor, you must have faith in active favor in your life, and when favor comes you will know it, because it will distinguish you.

In looking at the subject of Favor, it starts all the way back with Noah in Genesis 6:5-8;

> "And GOD saw that the wickedness of man *was* great in the earth, and *that* every imagination of the thoughts of his heart *was* only evil continually. ₆ And it repented the LORD that he had made man on the earth, and it grieved him at his heart. ₇ And the LORD said, I will destroy man whom I have created from the face of the earth; both man, and beast, and the creeping thing, and the fowls of the air; for it repenteth me that I have made them. ₈ But Noah found grace (Favor) in the eyes of the LORD." (*Genesis 6:5-8 Emphasis adds*)

The word grace means 'Favor', as you know and see from the scriptures that God picked Noah out, while others perish, Noah and his family were sparred (Saved). Favor will cause you to be sparred while others fall by the wayside. As you continue to examine the scriptures and track the lives of various people who are successful and you will see it was because of the Favor of God in their lives.

When you understand Favor, and lay claim of the promise of Favor, and expect Favor you will see that it is the key to your being brought to the top, see Favor is the way to the top.

Just a reminder that righteousness or right standing with God is required in order to be a candidate for Favor, and in the Kingdom of God you are expected to rise to the top, and unlike the kingdom of darkness they want to hold you back, but Favor can turn it all that around.

There are several verses that you need to examine in light of Favor, Genesis 39:1; Proverbs 24:5,10; and Luke 4:5-8, See Favor is the way to the top, when God promotes you there is not a demon, a government that can stop you. See true promotion comes from God.

Favor will open up an opportunity, we have the example of Joseph and Daniel went from slave to heir to Egypt. (See Psalms 30:5)

Some people do not put value on Favor, because they do not realize what it is, or what it can do.

What does Favor mean to you and me? Favor comes directly from God; I do not have to beg someone to do something for me. I do not have to bow down or compromise myself of my beliefs to get a door open, the only thing that I need to know is that Favor is on my life.

See Favor determines the limit on everyone's destiny, it is not going to happen without some Favor, God gives divine Favor.

It is seen here that God is willing to bless the righteous and also protect them with the weapon of favor. When the favor of God is upon a man, he will be secured and protected against all oppositions and anti-favor moves of men.

> 'For You; O Jehovah, will bless the righteous; with favor You will surround him as with a shield.'
> Psalms 5:12

When you find favor with God, suddenly, whatever you touch begins to prosper and people will begin to wonder how? Divine Favor can give you just one contact and all of a sudden for the rest of your life you can enjoy.

Some additional verses that you need to examine in light of Favor, remember 'Grace of God, is the Favor of God'

Joseph, because of favor:

- Everything he touched prospered, even in prison. When they took him to prison, very soon he became the man in charge. Genesis 39:21-23.
- He was referred to here by Pharaoh and Pharaoh said, "there is none as wise as thou art" Joseph found favor with God. (Genesis 41:39).
- "God has made me Lord of all Egypt." and he sent to his father and he said, "Come with all your family. I will feed you for the rest of your life." (Genesis 45:4-13)
- In the home of Joseph there was peace, there was harmony. He had 2 sons everything anybody could want in a home was there – he didn't even have to look for a wife – one was given him! He had favor! Genesis 48:8-20

Moses, because of favor:

- Moses found the favor of God at the backside of the desert. Then Moses said to the LORD, "See, You say to me, 'Bring up this people!' But You Yourself have not let me know whom You will send with me. Moreover, You have said, 'I have known you by name, and you have also found favor in My sight.' 13"Now therefore, I pray You, if I have found favor in Your sight, let me know Your ways that I may know You, so that I may find favor in Your sight. Consider, too, that this nation is Your people. (Exodus 33:12-14)

Esther, because of favor:

She was selected among several other beautiful ladies that are qualified to be the queen. Esther 2: 15-17, Esther found Favor before the King. (Esther 5:1-3).

David, because of favor:

He was the most unqualified person naturally in his family, but God rejected others to look for him. 1 Samuel 16: 11-13. Divine favor singled out for a miracle. (2 Kings 5:1-14).

When David found favor with God, the boy who was despised by his relatives, the one whom they would never have been presented for election to be king, became a celebrated person. Up till today we still talk about David.

Daniel, because of favor:

We can see this kind of favor operating in the life of Daniel. He and all the Israelites were prisoners in Babylon. For reasons that cannot be explained naturally, though, he had favor with the leaders of the land.

> "Now God had brought Daniel into favor and tender love with the prince of the eunuchs" (Daniel 1:9).

In other accounts we learn that Daniel had so much favor with the leaders of the land, he was elevated to prestigious positions in The Babylonian Kingdom. Even though the circumstances were stacked against him, Daniel eventually became the prime minister of Babylon.

Wisdom belongs to God and He gives wisdom to the wise. (Daniel 2:20-22)

The favor of God will single you out for a miracle. The Bible says Jesus came to Jericho and as he was coming out of Jericho, a great multitude followed him! A multitude followed Him! But how many of the people in the multitude got a miracle? Only blind Bartemeus who was by the highway side begging! (Mark 10:46-52)

The Bible says whoso findeth a wife, findeth a good thing and obtains favor of God. If you have no husband you'll get a husband. (Amen!) If you have no wife you'll get a wife. If you are barren, you'll have children. (Amen!) (Proverbs 18:22)

How can I get the Favor of God in my life?

> "Thou shalt also decree a thing, and it shall be established unto thee: and the light shall shine upon thy ways". Job 22:28

Make a demand on the Favor of God in your life every day. You decree it, you speak it out. You get up in the morning saying, "The Favor of God goes before me today." Throughout your day, whenever you think about it, you decree the Favor of God. Before you go to bed at night, you decree the Favor of God. Do not leave your house without decreeing the Favor of God. That is as natural to me as putting my clothes on before I leave the house.

By consistently decreeing God's Favor and speaking out that truth, we will see it manifest in our lives-bringing us the promotions, the raises, the open doors-we will see relationships, circumstances and situations changed to our benefit- there will be battles won that we don't even have to fight because God's Favor will win them for us.

Father, In the name of Jesus
- I am the righteousness of God and God's Favor surrounds the righteous.
- It surrounds me. It's all over me. It goes before me.
- I can depend upon it every day of my life.
- I decree out of my mouth that the Favor of God is opening doors that no man can shut.
- The Favor of God is changing things that even look impossible.
- The Favor of God is working in my behalf.
- Thank you, Father, in advance, for all the turnarounds, all the miracles, and all the breakthroughs that are coming my way because I have Favor with you. Amen
- I decree from this moment forward,
- I see myself the way God sees me.
- I am highly Favored of the Lord.
- I am crowned with glory and honor.
- I am the righteousness of God in Christ,
- I reigning as a King in life through the one man Jesus Christ the Messiah.
- I declare by faith that I walk in divine Favor.
- I have preferential treatment, supernatural increase, restoration, increased assets, great victories, recognition, prominence, petitions granted, policies and rules changed.

- Battles won I do not have to fight, all because of the Blessing and Favor of God on my life.

- Every morning when I rise, I expect divine Favor to go before me and surround me as with a shield with good will and pleasures forevermore. Doors are now open for me that men say are impossible to open. No obstacle can stop me, and no hindrances can delay me.

- I am honored by my Father, as I receive genuine Favor that comes directly from Him. I am special to Him. I am the object of His affection. I am blessed and highly Favored of the Lord, in Jesus' Name. Amen.

How to lose the Divine Favor of God?

If we go through the Bible very well, we shall review what some people did that attracted the favor of God upon their lives, and what others did that separated them from the favor of God. The following factors will destroy the favor of God in a man's life:

1) Disobedience to God - Saul enjoyed the favor of God and was selected as the first King of Israel, but through disobedience, he lost the divine favor. 1Samuel 15: 19-24

2) Sexual Sin - We saw Samson losing the favor of God due to his immoral lifestyle. All kinds of sexual sins and immoral lifestyle will make a man lose the favor of God. Judges 16: 18-21.

3) Pride - The devil (satan) was the anointed Cherub at the throne of God. He lost the highly placed position due to pride. God will give grace (favor inclusive) to the humble, but will resist a proud person. Naaman was almost losing the favor of his selective miracle due to pride, but was able to retain it when he humbled himself.

4) Stinginess and Lack of Giving - Those that know how to give are always abounding with the favor of God. Both the widow of Zarephath and the Shunammite woman received divine favor because they gave sacrificially. God said he will open the windows of heaven upon those that are faithful in their tithes and offerings. Malachi 3:8-12.

5) Lack of Faithfulness in the Service of God - If a man is faithful in the service of God, he will enjoy Divine Favor. Noah was faithful and his family was favorably preserved. The wife of the late prophet enjoyed Divine Favor due to the faithfulness of her husband in God's service.

6) Sowing the seed of Wickedness - The door of favor shall be shot against anyone sowing the seed of wickedness against others. A man will reap what he sows. Adonibezek has been cutting the fingers and toes of other kings without mercy, until it happened to him one day. Judges 1: 5-7.

7) Prayerlessness - Prayer remains one the most effective keys that unlock the door of favor. When Esther prayed, she found favor before the king; likewise Nehemiah prayed and received favor.

Summary

God's favor can bring a lot of blessings upon a man. Divine favors can:

- Produce supernatural promotion and increase (Genesis 39:21)
- Bring restoration of everything the enemy has stolen (Exodus 3:21).
- Bring honor in the midst of adversaries (Exodus 11:3).
- Produce increased assets (Deuteronomy 33:23).
- Give great and unusual victories even against impossible odds (Joshua 6:20; 10: 9, 20).

- Give recognition, promotion even when it's least likely one to receive it (1 Samuel. 16:22).
- Produce prominence and preferential treatment, Favor and kindness (Esther 5:8).
- Get petitions granted, even by the ungodly civil authority (Esther 5:8).
- Change rules, regulations, even laws, if necessary to your advantage (Esther 8:5).
- Win battles you did not even have to fight. God will fight them for you (Psalm 44:3).

To receive Favor, there is a price to be paid, and that is righteousness. It comes through the new birth and through continuing in total obedience to the word of God. In prayer, we can lay hold of God's promises in His words and the door of favor shall be opened unto us.

The Law of Confession

"Death and life *are* in the power of the tongue: and they that love it shall eat the fruit thereof." Proverbs 18:21

Chapter Fifteen
The Law of Confession

Purpose

There is power in the words that we speak. We reap what we sow and words are seeds. Therefore, if the words we speak are negative, then we reap negativity. And, if we speak words that are positive, then we reap positivity.

Everything that's happening in your life right now; being good or bad is the result of words. Not just your words. It could be words from family members, friends, teachers, etc. Even if there are undesirable situations you are dealing with; just remember that words can also turn situations around.

The Power of Words - The universe we live in functions based upon laws and principles; such as the law of attraction, the law of gravity, and etc. God created the universe to function that way. Jesus said... I will give you the keys to the kingdom (Matthew 16:19)

One way to operate this law in Yoking up with Jesus is learning the value of Words, especially the Word of God. Many Christians don't understand the law of Confession. One way a couple becomes one is by saying the same thing. So one way of Yoking up with Jesus is by valuing and speak only what thus saith the Lord, the Word of God.

In Matthew 13:17-19 Jesus says

> "...**17**For verily I say unto you, that many prophets and righteous men have desired to see those things which ye see, and have not seen them; and to hear those things which ye hear, and have not heard them. **18**Hear ye therefore the parable of the sower **19**When any one heareth the word of the kingdom, and understandeth it not, then cometh the wicked one, and catcheth away that which was sown in his heart. This is he which received seed by the way side God created this universe with the words that He spoke and likewise, you were made to manifest every word that you speak. There is power in your words and you will have what you say whether it is good or bad... so watch your mouth.

For Example, in the book of Daniel, Nebuchadnezzar, King of Babylon, had made a law that everyone must fall down and worship the golden statue when the music starting playing. There were three Hebrews who were among the Jews in Babylonian captivity, who were defiant, saying in Daniel 3:18, "... "We will not serve thy gods nor worship the golden image which thou has set up".

They were refusing to serve the gods of the Babylonians because it conflicted with the law of their God, Jehovah which said, in Exodus 20:2-5 "..."Thou shall have no other gods before me... thou shall not bow down thyself to them, nor serve them" Thus, the three Hebrews in refusing to bow, chose to live by the Word of God in their hearts rather than the written laws of a heathen nation.

They believed and decreed their deliverance, saying, "… Our God whom we serve is able to deliver us from the burning fiery furnace, and He will deliver us out of thy hand, O king."

And, as it was expected, He did. Supernaturally! They were living by the Word of God in their hearts instead of an external system.

Now you can understand what David wrote, Psalm 119:11 says "… Thy word have I hid in my heart, that I might not sin against thee" Another example of this "Kingdom living," or living from the inside out, is found in the New Testament, in the Gospel according to Mark 4:35-41.

Notice what Jesus used to stop the storm? In Matthew 12:34; He released words. Where did these words come from? From the Father and were stored in His Heart. "Out of the abundance of the heart the mouth speaketh. Oh, He could do that because He was God in the flesh." That's true, but Jesus sat His Godhead abilities aside and functioned in this earth as a man anointed by God. Paul called Him the last Adam. They said, "What manner of man is this that even the wind and the sea obey Him."

In the book of Proverbs it tells us that, "Death and life are in the power of the tongue: and they that love it shall eat the fruit thereof. Notice what it didn't say. It didn't say death and life are in the power of the devil. Neither did it say in the power of God. No, It said, "Death and life are in the power of the tongue," that includes "your tongue." Jesus, being controlled by the Word of God on the inside of Him, spoke life to this situation.

The disciple, on the other hand, under pressure of the raging storm spoke death, saying, "… We're all about to drown."

How many of us believers have done this same thing? We have operated under the control of external circumstances and not by God's Word. Remember, words are seeds in the spirit realm. And, they are programmed to produce a harvest of whatever is sown. You may have something in your life that you want to be rid of. It might be poverty, failures, sickness, or a feeling of inferiority.

Whatever it is that you have in your life are harvested or the manifestation of seeds that have been sown. Nothing, just happens. It could be your words, words of your parents, your teachers, your close friends, or words sown into your grandmother and passed on to you in the form of how you were trained. The bottom line is, where you are now is the result of somebody's words.

Speak the Words only! - In the book of Proverbs 18:21 it tells us that, "Death and life are in the power of the tongue: and they that love it shall eat the fruit thereof" In Proverbs 26:22 the words of a talebearer are as wounds, and they go down into the innermost parts of the belly.

Let us examine this principle a bit closer. Every word we speak is a seed and if conceived or planted in the soil of the heart (spirit) will bring forth a harvest"… after his kind" (Genesis 1:11) From the beginning, starting with Adam and Eve, God never intended for mankind to speak anything he or she didn't want or believe that it would come to pass. I read where a man said that God told him, "instead of my people having what they say, they are saying what they have".

> "Thou art snared with the words of thy mouth; thou art taken with the words of thy mouth."
>
> (Proverbs 6:2)

> "In the multitude of words there wanteth not sin: but he that refraineth his lips is wise." (Proverbs 10:19)

I read another statement where a man who needed surgery. He kept saying to his relatives and to the physician, "if I have to undergo an operation, I know I'll die."

Guess what? The doctor refused to operate. He knew the power of words.

> Joel said…"Let the weak say, I am strong" (Joel 3:10).

> 2 Corinthians 4:18 - ¹⁸While we look not at the things which are seen, but at the things which are not seen: for the things which are seen are temporal; but the things which are not seen are eternal.

> Romans 4:17 - As it is written, I have made thee a father of many nations, before him whom he believed, even God, who quickeneth the dead, and calleth those things which be not as though they were.

The Law of confession

God created this universe with the words that He spoke and likewise, you were made to manifest every word that you speak. There is power in your words and you will have what you say whether it is good or bad… so watch your mouth.

Jesus came preaching the Kingdom of God. He was reintroducing the Kingdom of God to man, bringing us back up to where mankind was before the fall, ruling this earth with words.

I call it Kingdom Living, "Kingdom living" is simply living by the Word of God in our hearts rather than under the control of an external system or circumstance.

Three examples that will explain the law of confession: The law of Confession means to speak the same thing that God says:

Jesus said…"
> For verily I say unto you, that whosoever shall say unto this mountain, be thou removed, and be thou cast into the sea; and shall not doubt in his heart, but shall believe that those things which he saith shall come to pass; he shall have whatsoever he saith.
> (Mark 11:23)

Jesus said unto him, "if thou canst believe, all things are possible to him that believeth." (Mark 9:23)

In order to show you exactly how law of Confession works we are given examples within the scriptures:

> "²For in many things we offend all. If any man offend not in word, the same is a perfect man, and able also to bridle the whole body. ³Behold, we put bits in the horses' mouths that they may obey us; and we turn about their whole body. "(James 3:2, 3)

The way that mankind has tamed and controlled horses is by placing a bit in their mouths; The way that the riders is able to control, and have the horse to go in the direction that he or she desires to go is by applying pressure on the tongue of the horse. When you desire for the horse to turn right you pull on the side of the bit. But, perhaps you didn't know this and just thought that it was just pulling against the horse's jaw. No, when you pull on the bit you are actually putting pressure on the horse's tongue. It is the tongue that causes the whole body to turn.

Initially, when the bit is placed in the horses' mouth, it will show some resistance to the pressure, but as the rider continues to apply the pressure you will notice that the whole body becomes subject to that pressure and began to cooperate with the rider.

Another illustration is found in

James 3:4 says…

> "⁴Behold also the ships, which though they be so great, and are driven of fierce winds, yet are they turned about with a very small helm, whithersoever the governor listeth."

I don't know about you, but I have seen some cruise ships and they are pretty big, and when the Captain needs to turn the ship in a certain direction he doesn't jump into the water and turn the ship in the direction that he wasn't it to go. There is a steering wheel at the front of the ship. The entire steering apparatus of a ship's steering wheel is attached to a rudder (fore-and-after line) that causes the ship to turn the number of degrees by applying pressure to the rubber.

James 3:5-6 says…

> "⁵Even so the tongue is a little member, and boasteth great things. Behold how great a matter a little fire kindleth! ⁶And the tongue is a fire, a world of iniquity: so is the tongue among our members, that it defileth the whole body, and setteth on fire the course of nature; and it is set on fire of hell."

I remember when I was a young child my dad would get up early in the morning and start a fire in a pot belly stove. When we got up it was nice and warm. When my dad got up very early in the morning the house would be extremely cold and after the fire gets going the house would begin to get comfortable. Once my brother and I got older we were responsible for getting kindling and wood for our heating system back then.

My brother and I would go down in the woods and look for wood that was very dry and wood that had sapped on it. Sap is a syrupy type substance and great for starting a fire, because once the kindling was lit and burning it would cause the other wood to catch afire. The kindling was the littlest member in the stove, but once it got started it would cause everything to catch afire. Think about all of the problems or issues that you have had in life, It has been because of your tongue or somebody else tongue.

Proverbs 18:8 and 26:22 says…

> " The words of a talebearer are as wounds, and they go down into the innermost parts of the belly."

You may have something in your life that you want to be rid of. It might be poverty, failure, sickness, or a feeling of inferiority. Whatever it is in your life; good or bad, are harvested or the manifestation of seeds that have been sown.

Again, everything happens for a reason.

It could be your words, words of your parents, your teachers, your close friends, or words sown into your grandmother and passed on to you in the form of how you were trained. The bottom line is, where you are now is the result of somebody's words. There are no situations that you can't turn around with words.

Make this confession over your life

> In Christ I am anointed and a powerful person of God. I am a joint-heir with Jesus and more than a conqueror. I am a doer of the Word of God and a channel for His blessings. If God is for me, who can be against me?

The Mystery of Confession - Spiritual Law - God and His creation operate according to spiritual laws. These laws cannot be violated and when properly used these spiritual laws will always produce the desired results.

"We must understand that there are laws governing every single thing in existence. Nothing is by accident. There are laws of the world of the spirit, and there are laws of the world of the natural. We need to realize that the spiritual world and its laws are more powerful than the physical world and its laws.

Spiritual laws gave birth to physical laws. . . God a Spirit, created all matters. . . with the force of faith.

Positive Confession - God creates by confessing what He wants. We are created in His image, thus we too have the ability to release faith-filled words and thus create what we need in life. Spiritual law generally works by confessing properly what you need. If you need physical healing you confess passages of text on prosperity.

The "spiritual law" is simple
- (1) Believe in your heart,
- (2) Confess it with your mouth, and
- (3) Believe you have **it** and you will see the manifestation of **it**.

"What you are believe that you receive" (Mark 11:23-24).

"Even though God had the image inside Him and the Spirit of God was there to cause it to come to pass, it had to be released out of His mouth before any changes could take place. God used His words to bring the image into manifestation. He filled His words with the spiritual force of faith."

The High Priest of Our Confession

Very few believers today understand the mystery of the Apostleship and Priesthood of Jesus. We think that an apostle is some kind of super saint. But "apostle" actually means, "Sent one." So, Jesus has been sent from God to do something for us. He's been sent to serve as our High Priest.

Again, many believers don't have the first idea what a high priest does. They picture a person walking around in strange clothes performing religious rituals.

In reality, a high priest is much more than that. He is one who is authorized to administer, to execute, or to carry out on your behalf.

Hebrews 3:1 says

> "Wherefore, holy brethren, partakers of the heavenly calling, consider the Apostle and High Priest of our profession, Christ Jesus;" He's been sent to put into effect, to carry out the words that you say. (Isaiah 55:8-11, Psalm 103:20, Hebrews 1:14)

Question - Have you been speaking, what you feel, instead of speaking words of faith? If, for example, you're speaking sickness, what He going do with that? He's not a High Priest over sickness.

He can't execute that. If you're saying, "I'm so weak, I'm so tired," He can't carry that out. The Bible says, "Let the weak say, I am strong!" The minute you say that, Jesus can administer STRENGTH.

Jesus is not going to administer sickness or disease or poverty or sin. He's defeated all that. He is High Priest over deliverance and righteousness and freedom. Consider that, and then as you come before Jesus, don't speak words of defeat. Speak words He can implement the words of victory. That's what He's been ordained by God to bring to pass in your life. Many people fail to receive what they pray for because of lack of understanding about confession.

Again in Hebrews 3:1 we are commanded to "consider Christ Jesus the Apostle and High Priest of our confession." As our High Priest, Jesus acts in our behalf according to what we confess when it is in accordance with God's Word.

Examples: – Jacob / Rachel, Genesis 31:30-32 and 35:17- 19; Gabriel / Zachariah – Luke 1:1 -24;

The devil knows! - In Genesis 3:1-7 now the serpent was craftier than any of the wild animals the LORD God had made. He said to the woman, "Did God really say, 'You must not eat from any tree in the garden'?" The woman said to the serpent, "We may eat fruit from the trees in the garden, but God did say, 'You must not eat fruit from the tree that is in the middle of the garden, and you must not touch it, or you will die.'

"You will not surely die," the serpent said to the woman. "God knows that when you eat of it your eyes will be opened, and you will be like God, knowing good and evil."

When the woman saw that the fruit of the tree was good for food and pleasing to the eye, and also desirable for gaining wisdom, she took some and ate it. She also gave some to her husband, who was with her, and he ate it. Then the eyes of both of them were opened, and they realized they were naked; so they sewed fig leaves together and made coverings for themselves.

What happened? The Fall of Man; it is important for us to understand how the devil tricked Adam and Eve into disobeying God. Military intelligence on enemy tactics is crucial in a war. We are in a spiritual war until Jesus comes back. Therefore, we must understand the tactics of the enemy if we are to be successful in daily battles. Paul taught us that we should not be unaware of the devil's tactics in 2 Corinthians 2:11. With that in mind, let's take a closer look at his tactics:

Changing God's Word - The first thing that the enemy did was to cast doubt on what God said. He attacked God's command and attempted to twist God's Words. This is why it is so very important for us to know and understand the Word of God for ourselves. (Matthew 13:28-31). The bible speaks of false prophets coming to lead many astray. Most people are led astray, like Eve was, because they allow someone to come and confuse them about the Word of God.

We need to clearly understand the Word of God and how it applies to our daily lives. The father or Lies: John taught us that the devil is a liar and the father of it (John 8:44). He uses lies to deceive people daily.

In the text, he told Eve that:

(1) She would not die and that,

(2) If she ate of the fruit, her eyes would be opened and she would, be like God. The problem here is that God told Eve she would die (spiritually). Furthermore, she was already like God.

(3) We must learn why man was created? Man in His image and likeness and gave man dominion in the earth. Man has been already like God and this act would actually cause the separation between God and man.

The Big Three: Towards the end of the book, John teaches us to stay away from what I call 'The Big Three.' He said, (1 John 2:16) For all that is in the world, the lust of the flesh, and the lust of the eyes, and the pride of life, is not of the Father, but is of the world. We now go back to the beginning of the book and find the same three tactics.

The text says when the woman saw that the fruit of the tree was good for food (the lust of the flesh) and pleasing to the eye (the lust of the eyes), and also desirable for gaining wisdom (the pride of life), she took some and ate it.

Summary

These are the same three tactics that the devil uses against us daily and the sad part is that we keep falling for them.

(1) We need to know the Word of God and not allow anyone to twist God's Word and lead us astray.

(2) We must recognize that the devil is the father of lies and realize that he will consistently attack us through lying.

(3) We must understand the 'Big Three' tactics of the devil and make every attempt not to allow ourselves to be caught by them.

The Sample prayer of Agreement

Again I say unto you, that if two of you shall agree on earth as touching anything that they shall ask, it shall be done for them of my Father which is in heaven. Matthew 18:19

Chapter Sixteen
A Sample Prayer of Agreement

The prayer of agreement when prayed according to Matthew 18:18-20 will cover every circumstance in life.

> "Verily I say unto you, whatsoever ye shall bind on earth shall be bound in heaven: and whatsoever ye shall loose on earth shall be loosed in heaven. Again I say unto you, that if two of you shall agree on earth as touching anything that they shall ask, it shall be done for them of my Father which is in heaven. For where two or three are gathered together in my name, there am I in the midst of them."

Let me use finances to illustrate. The first thing to do is agree with the Word. Read the scriptures and pray. I write down our agreements like this: "We hereby agree, according to Philippians 4:19 and Matthew 18:19 as follows: 'Father, we see in Your Word that You will supply all our needs according to Your riches in glory.

We are setting ourselves in agreement that our financial need is met according to Your Word. We believe we receive (be specific) _____. We set ourselves in agreement, and we believe we receive now, and we praise You for it. We establish this agreement, in Jesus' Name. Amen.'

(Signature)   (Date)

(Signature)   (Date)

Amen means "So be it." As far as we are concerned, the matter is closed. We just thank God from that point forward. We know if we want results *we must not waver*. To waver is to doubt.

If the devil brings doubt, we simply speak to him on the authority of Jesus' Name, and say, "Don't bring us your lies. Not only is it written in God's Word, but we have agreed. We have written it down." As far as we are concerned, the need is met. There is no doubt about it because we have agreed, according to the Word of God. Consequently, our confession and actions will be in line with what we have established as truth.

There have been times when we have wavered, so we take it to God and receive forgiveness for unbelief, reinforce our original decree and go at it again. We all make mistakes in the walk of faith. The important thing is to keep walking. If you miss it, go at it again. The biggest mistake of all is to become discouraged and quit before you receive your answer.

I challenge you to write down your agreements. Seeing it in black and white on paper will make a difference! You will be more likely to line up your confession and your actions with your agreement. Jesus said that if any two on earth agree, He would be in the midst of that agreement to see that it comes to pass. You are on earth, so you qualify. If you agree with another believer as touching anything that lines up with the Word of God, He is there in your midst to carry it out.

Jesus wants you to agree and will see to it that it comes to pass. The word *agrees* is translated in *The Amplified Bible* as "agree and harmonize together or make a symphony together."

The word symphony has a meaning that is imperative to our subject, it means "all available instruments in harmony." You must have your spirit, mind and actions in agreement with the Word. Agreeing spiritually is to agree with the Word of God. Make up your mind God's Word is true and that it will come to pass.

Secondly, be strong in your mind. That is the devil battleground. You must control your thoughts. Writing down your agreement will be beneficial for this reason. It will keep it before your eyes so when your mind tries to change directions, control it with your agreement with God's Word. Do not tie God's hands. Allow Him to work. You agree, spirit and soul (mind).

Then your actions must come in line. If finances are what you agreed on, expect the money to come in. This is part of being in agreement. You cannot agree in prayer about something, then act the opposite and expect it to come to pass. If you do, your actions will eventually take over your thinking.

Agreement with the Word and another believer are not the only things involved in this kind of prayer. Agreement is also harmony.

Harmony is extremely important. When speaking of prayer in Mark 11:25-26, Jesus said, "And when ye stand praying, forgive, if ye have aught against any: that your Father also which is in heaven may forgive you your trespasses. But if ye do not forgive, neither will your Father which is in heaven forgive your trespasses." This is vital in your prayer life. You must forgive everyone who has offended you.

Jesus did not say, *"Think about it for six weeks and then forgive if or when you feel better."* He said, *forgive when you pray.*

Jesus prayed, "Our Father which art in heaven, Hallowed be thy name. Thy kingdom come, Thy will be done in earth, as it is in heaven. Give us this day our daily bread. And forgive us our debts, as we forgive our debtors" (Matthew 6:9-12). He put a condition on forgiveness. The condition is "I don't expect to be forgiven until I forgive." He displayed the kind of discipline the believer should exercise when he is praying.

How important is this? In Galatians 5:6, the Bible says faith works by love. If you are operating with an unforgiving heart, your prayer life will be paralyzed. The Word says we know we have the petitions we have desired of Him, if we do the things that are pleasing in His sight (I John 3:22). Put these scriptures together and you quickly see unforgiveness would actually ruin the whole prayer system.

The agreement makes prayer work. You can experience a place of agreement with God's Word, and harmony that will produce power, as you forgive and agree with another believer. You can affect governments, families and the lives of others. You can change your financial situation; affect your church and your pastor with the power of prayer. Find someone who can agree with you according to the Word of God.

The same principle works the other way. If you are in *dis*agreement, the door is open for Satan to come in. "For where envying and strife is, there is confusion and every evil work" (James 3:16).

In Matthew 18:21, Peter asked Jesus, "Lord, how oft shall my brother sin against me, and I forgive him? Till seven times? Jesus replied, "I say not unto thee, until seven times: but, until seventy times seven.

How many times shall I forgive my brother when he sins against me? Up to seven times?" Jesus replied, "I tell you, not seven times, but until seventy times seven" (verse 22). Forgive because God said to, and not because you feel like it. Build your home, your church and every other area of your life in the unselfish love of God. Selfishness have never built anything it did not destroy. But love never fails.

Summary

The love of God is the very center of the family of God because God is love. You are His very own child, born again with His love nature inside you. Don't let that love lie dormant. Cast down selfishness and let loose the love of God in you. You cannot fail when love is in dominion.

When you forgive and reach for harmony, you come to a place where you have the spiritual awareness to perceive the closeness of God. Jesus said if you get into harmony and agree together, He would be in the midst of you. God wants to be involved with you.

When you are in harmony and agreement with those around you, you will step into a deeper, more personal fellowship with God. He becomes real and vital to you. Fellowship with your heavenly Father is one of the greatest things you will ever have in your Christian walk!

It causes a confidence and an assurance deep down in your heart. You know your prayers are answered because you have conformed yourself to His will. As you forgive, the joy that comes through answered prayer will become your own personal experience. Jesus said, "Ask, and ye shall receive, that your joy may be full" (John 16:24).

The Prayer of Faith

"And the prayer of faith shall save the sick, and the Lord shall raise him up; and if he have committed sins, they shall be forgiven him." James 5:15

Chapter Seventeen
Sample Prayer of Faith for Finances

Purpose

The prayer of faith is a "prayer that changes things." Please note that it changes things and not people. Too often we try to help someone by praying that they change their behavior. But people do not change against their will. What people need is to recognize their need for God and to give their life to Him. Once they do that, then God can show them what He wants them to be and give them the ability to change.

The prayer of faith changes things or circumstances. Anything that can be seen is subject to change and can be affected by a prayer of faith.

According to 2 Corinthians 4:18 (NKJV)

> "While we do not look at the things which are seen, but at the things which are not seen. For the things which are seen *are* temporary, but the things which are not seen *are* eternal."

The prayer of faith changes things like physical ailments, lack of wisdom, or your employment status. Through the prayer of faith, you can receive healing and health for your body, wisdom for your mind, and even a good job. Before you get the wrong idea, the prayer of faith is not a magic wand or a genie in a bottle. But the prayer of faith is a tool that we can use to implement God's will in our lives.

Through the prayer of faith, we can receive the things that God desires for us to have. God desires us to be healthy, wise, and gainfully employed, etc. Although these good things may not be a reality in your life right now, with the prayer of faith, these things that you are hoping for can become reality. When you pray the Prayer of Faith for prosperity, you are not asking for things that are not His will. Make sure that you ask in line with His Word. Don't just say things that sound spiritual or religious. Say what His Word says. Also, be sure to pray for finances that will help further the kingdom of God.

You might be on the verge of losing your house. You might be on the verge of losing your church. You might be on the verge of losing all that you have saved over the years. You have the right to pray for financial blessing. If you are in a place today where you need God to step in and help your financial situation, here is a prayer for you.

Sample Prayer of Faith for Finances

Heavenly Father, Be it known this day, _____ (A.M/P.M.), that I receive a heavenly Financial blessing in the amount of $ _____. **Heavenly Father**, in the name of Jesus, I come boldly to the throne of grace, and present Your Word. According to John 16:23, Jesus said, "And in that day you will ask Me nothing.

Most assuredly, I say to you, whatever you ask the Father in My name He will give you. (John 16:23 NKJV) Jesus, You said in Mark 11:24, "Therefore I say to you, whatever things you ask when you pray, believe that you receive *them,* and you will have *them.* (Mark 11:24 NKJV)

Your Word states in Luke 6:38, "Give, and it will be given to you: good measure, pressed down, shaken together, and running over will be put into your bosom. For with the same measure that you use, it will be measured back to you." (Luke 6:38 NKJV)

In accordance with Your Word, I give and I sow seed, in order to set this spiritual law to work on my behalf. Because l am a cheerful (joyous, 'prompt to do it) giver [whose heart is in his giving], "[7] So let each one give as he purposes in his heart, not grudgingly or of necessity; for God loves a cheerful giver. [8] And God is able to make all grace abound toward you, that you, always having all sufficiency in all things, may have an abundance for every good work. (2 Corinthians 9:7-8 NKJV *with personal paraphrase*).

According to Matthew 18:18, I bind the devil and all his cohorts, and I render them helpless and unable to operate against me. They will not hinder my Heavenly Financial blessing. According to Hebrews 1:13-14, I loose the ministering spirits, and I charge them to go forth and cause my request to come into my hands. I have applied for this Heavenly Financial blessing for the following:

Agreement (when appropriate): Jesus, You said in Matthew 18:19, "Again I say unto you, that if two of you shall agree on earth as touching anything that they shall ask, it shall be done for them of my Father which is in heaven."

Therefore, _____ and we set ourselves in agreement, and we believe we receive now, and we praise You for it.
(Signature) _____ (Date) _____

(Signature) _____ (Date) _____

Naming Your Seed

"For as the rain cometh down, and the snow from heaven, and returneth not thither, but watereth the earth, and maketh it bring forth and bud, that it may give seed to the sower, and bread to the eater:" (Isaiah 55:10; 2 Corinthians 9:6-10)

Chapter Eighteen
Naming Your Seed

Purpose

Why Struggle when it is not necessary? Of course, since the beginning of time man has had to work. This came about when Adam and Eve failed God by being disobedient. But, even so, we still do not have to work as hard if we apply the kingdom of God laws and principle in our daily living.

In order to learn and understand the Kingdom of God laws, one must read their bible. The bible has all of the answers that are needed so that we can live a blessed life instead of a stressed life. This chapter will teach the three steps to take in our lives in order to receive the blessing of the Kingdom of God.

NAMING YOUR SEED - Money can be used for multiplying your needs. We also use the money for bartering. Money represents our life, and it is valuable. When you sow it you are to name your seed based upon whatever your situation calls for and confess the Word of God and stand on it.

In the operation of this basic principle - sowing and reaping;

> Galatians 6:7
> "7Be not deceived; God is not mocked: for whatsoever a man soweth, that shall he also reap."

Whatever you put in the ground is going to come up. Whatsoever encompasses all human activity? All of our acts are forces. Every time we think, every time we feel, every time we exercise our will, we are sowing. Therefore, we have to consider our ways and give thought to what we are sowing. If you consider what you are sowing, then you will recognize your harvest.

2 Corinthians 9:10 AMP

> "And God Who provides seed for the sower and bread for eating will also provide and multiply your resources for sowing and increase the fruits of your righteousness which manifests itself in active goodness, kindness, and charity"

One of the most powerful laws to ever govern the earth is the law of sowing and reaping. It is what God established in the beginning.

Genesis 8:22;

> "22While the earth remaineth, seedtime and harvest, and old and heat, and summer and winter, and day and night shall not cease."

It is one the most powerful law, yet it is a law that is often misunderstood. This law should be understood the most because of its multifaceted nature. Just as we are aware of the law of gravity, we should be just as aware of this law of sowing and reaping.

Our main priority under this law and as a child of God is to make sure it is working in our favor. It should always work in our favor, and in understanding this law is that as long as you have seed you shouldn't ever lack anything.

What is a Seed?

A seed is anything that you have that can be sown, given, or planted into someone else; (words, kindness, generosity, favor, money, good deeds, and time), just to name a few. The Bible says that God gives seed to the sower. That means that a sower is never without seed as long as he or she is in covenant with God. The Bible is clear that God provides the seed. In other words, what is it that God gave you to be a blessing to others?

Isaiah 55:10;

> "¹⁰For as the rain cometh down, and the snow from heaven, and returneth not thither, but watereth the earth, and maketh it bring forth and bud, that it may give seed to the sower, and bread to the eater:"

2 Corinthians 9:10;

> "¹⁰Now he that ministereth seed to the sower both minister bread for your food, and multiply your seed sown, and increase the fruits of your righteousness;"

As I am sharing this with you I made this my main focus to receiving blessings from God. There was a time in my life when I was out of work, and the revenue was not coming in like I expected. I cleared my desk, and I got serious about being blessed, and I have been blessed, and I am blessed. I want to challenge you to do as I did, and work the Word of God. You don't have to be a part of the fallen world system. You can be a part of the Kingdom of God system where there is no lack. Where God is, there is pleasure and blessings for his citizens.

Psalm 16:11;

> "¹¹Thou wilt shew me the path of life: in thy presence is fullness of joy; at thy right hand there are pleasures for evermore."

Once you discover what it is that God has given you to sow, name it and sow it. What do you want the seed to do? Be specific in your prayers over your seed.

When you name it, claim the type of harvest you want to receive from it. Please know that as God gave Adam the seed of authority, remember that Jesus has given us authority as well. We must put it to use and expect an abundance of return as a harvest. Remember, you will reap what you sow.

Galatians 6:7;

> "⁷Be not deceived; God is not mocked: for whatsoever a man soweth, that shall he also reap."

Seedtime and harvest is just as much a financial law as it is a physical and a spiritual law. We have to understand that when it comes to giving finances toward God's Kingdom, we can fully expect to draw on the promises of God of Sowing and Reaping.

Name Your Seed – Isaiah 55:11 (specific need)

> "So shall my word be that goeth forth out of my mouth: it shall not return unto me void, but it shall accomplish that which I please, and it shall prosper *in the thing* whereto I sent it."

Summary

Often times when a person works and gain a paycheck, they think that they are supposed to live off their paycheck. In the world system a paycheck represents your world, and the world systems will only pay you enough to come back on Monday, the world system was never designed to pay you enough to get free of it. The amount you are paid by the world system is designed to keep you in bondage.

In order for us to live like God would have us to live, we must recognize that our paycheck is a seed. Sea in the Kingdom of God the paycheck is a seed, and after pay our tithes, give an offering, what we have left is SEED, and seed must be sown in order to reap a harvest and as we continue to do this the harvest will cause us to break free of the world systems.

Tracking Your Seed

"Let a man so account of us, as of the ministers of Christ, and stewards of the mysteries of God. ² Moreover it is required in stewards, that a man be found faithful. ³ But with me it is a very small thing that I should be judged of you, or of man's judgment: yea, I judge not mine own self."

1 Corinthians 4:1-3

Chapter Nineteen
Tracking your Seed

Purpose

This chapter will aid you in understanding how to Track Your seed from a spiritual perspective. Tracking is a feature that is available via the internet. The tracking feature gives details (date and time) of when a package will be delivered or received. You do not need the internet to track your seed as you do a package. In order to track your seed you need prayer and faith. In this chapter you will learn about praying the prayer of faith and the importance of sowing a seed. We must be obedient to God when sowing a seed and remember the Kingdom of God operates upon truth, honesty and integrity.

Recently I mailed a package at the local post office, and one of the options that were offered was tracking. When tracking a package via certified mail, log onto a computer, select the tracking option and confirm.

The tracking feature will give details of the exact date & time that a package will be delivered or an expected date of delivery. In other words, using a tracking feature allows you to know exactly when a package will be received. Briefly, in a couple paragraphs I will share two examples. Also, I will define several terms that will help us to understand tracking from a spiritual perspective.

Example: Step 1 Sowed, Step 2 Watering, and Step 3 Received. At one point in my life I wanted a 'Bose CD Player and CD Exchanger'. I PRAYED THE PRAYER OF FAITH AND believed and that I received it.

A) On October 14, 2010 (DATE AND TIME OF RELEASING YOUR FAITH); My 'Bose CD Player and CD Exchanger' and I sowed a seed of $40.00 into Bill Winston Ministries.

B) On March 11, 2011, (DATES OF WATERING MY SEED SOWN) I sowed another seed of $25.00 into Antioch Christians Center for my 'Bose CD Player and CD Exchanger that I believed I receive.

C) On June 9, 2011 (DATES OF WATERING MY SEED SOWN) I sowed another seed of $100.00 into the 700 Club for my 'Bose CD Player and CD Exchanger' that I believe that I receive.

D) On August 9, 2011 I sowed another seed of $20.00 into Christ for all nation ministries for my "Bose CD Player and CD Exchanger" that I believe that I receive.

E) On September 11, 2011, (DATES OF WATERING MY SEED SOWN) I sowed another seed of $100.00 into Pastor Naomi T. Hopkins of Refreshing Spring Christian Ministry, and I added a request for 3 CD's (Becoming, by Yolanda Adams, The Sound, by Mary & Mary, and Hello Fear, by Kirk Franklin.)

F) On October 27, 2011, (DATE HARVEST MANIFESTED) I received a check in the mail for $10,000.00 that cover the cost for the Bose CD Player and CD Exchanger ($749.00), the three CD's valued at ($45.00), plus the tithing from that harvest is always more than the amount of seeds sown ($285.00).

Again, I want you to know that God is faithful to His word, and as a child of God all we have to do is take Him at His word and act on it. Please know that God is not limited to the mail box, He manifests the harvest however He chooses. The Word works if you work it.

1. **Naming Your Seed (Money)** - Money can be used for multiplying your need. We use money for bartering. Money represents our life, and it is valuable. When you sow it you are to name your seed based upon whatever your situation calls for and confess the Word of God and standing on it.

2. **Scriptures You Are Standing On When Releasing Your Faith** – When we truly understand and operate kingdom laws and principles, God is obligated to his Word. We must have scriptures in order to know what God has promised. We can only lay claim on those promises through the knowledge of the Word of God. Within the Holy Bible, we have God promises; we claim them and apply them to our life

3. **Persons, Ministries, Or Organization (Ground) Seed Sown into** – A person, a ministry, or an organization must operate in truth, honesty and integrity.

The world system or the kingdom of darkness is a system that operates by deceptions, lies, and all types of corruptions. The Kingdom of God operates based upon truth, honesty and integrity. If a person, ministry, or an organization is not operating within these guidelines it would not be considered to be good ground. Remember, if the Holy Spirit is leading you to sow, just be obedient, because it is not always possible for us to know.

I remember one time I was watching a particular ministry, and I was about to sow into this ministry, but the Holy Spirit said "no".

4. **PRAYER OF AGREEMENT** - if you are married the scriptures says that your prayers can be hindered if spouses are not in agreement. If your spouse is not a Christian than it would be impossible for him/her to be in agreement, but the two of you must be in agreement. Please see chapter ten on the prayer of agreement.

5. **PRAY OF FAITH** - This prayer is when you present to God a list of what you are asking God for and believing that you receive them. From this point forward, thank God; and believe you received what you asked for until the manifestation of what you believe.

6. **DATE AND TIME OF RELEASING YOUR FAITH** - Write down and keep a note of the date and time you sowed your seed. I have asked this question of many Christians, "when was the last time you prayed for something specific and you received it"? Most of them did not know. That is why I suggest that you write down the date and time of your request.

7. **DATES OF WATERING SEED SOWN** - Once the prayer of faith is prayed, and the seed is sown, and while you are waiting for the manifestation of what you believe that you received, each time it crosses your mind, you should give God thanks by saying.

"Heavenly Father, I thank you that I believe that I receive", this is called watering your seed by giving thanks, praising, and worshipping God.

8. **DATE HARVEST (MANIFESTATION) WHAT YOU BELIEVED THAT YOU RECEIVE –** When the thing that you believe that you receive manifests, write the date and time and give praise and worship unto God that you now have it, and this ends this particular transaction with God.

Special Note: In tracking your seed, this mechanism is meant to be used as a tool that will help you be a good steward, managing what God has entrusted you with, but it is never meant to put limits on God, nor an attempt to buy a blessing.

YOU CAN MANAGE YOUR SEED BY TRACKING.

1. **Naming your seed (money)** – You sow it and name your seed based upon your need and confess the word of God.

2. **Scriptures (God's promises)** – God is obligated to his word. We claim them and apply them to our life.

3. **Sow a seed (ground)** – Based upon truth, honesty, and integrity.

4. **Prayer of agreement** – (when appropriate).

5. **Prayer of faith** – You ask God, you believe that you will receive. Thank God.

6. **Date and time of releasing your faith** – Write down the date and time of sowing your seed.

7. **Dates of watering seed sown** – Once the prayer of faith of is prayed and you're waiting on the manifestation, continue to give thanks, praise, and worship God.

8. **Manifestation** – What you believed that you will receive!

Yoking Up with Jesus and the Kingdom Government!

"Come unto me, all ye that labor and are heavy laden, and I will give you rest. ²⁹ Take my yoke upon you, and learn of me; for I am meek and lowly in heart: and ye shall find rest unto your souls. ³⁰ For my yoke is easy, and my burden is light.   *Matthew 11:28-30*

Chapter Twenty
Yoking up with Jesus and Kingdom of God Government

Winning in any area of life requires spiritual laws and understanding the Kingdom of God, We must gain the knowledge of God laws and obtaining wisdom on how to implement them into our lives. My life changed by applying the Kingdom of God laws and principles to my life situations.

When Jesus began His earthly ministry He announced the Kingdom of God is at hand and He began to preach repent for the kingdom of Heaven is at hand Matthew 4:17.

As seen from above scripture, Jesus came preaching and teaching about the Kingdom of God, and if we want to experience the blessing of the Kingdom of God while on earth we must yoke up with Jesus and the kingdom Laws and principles. Jesus said yoke up with me in the Kingdom of God laws and principles.

Matthew 11:28-30; Jesus said…"²⁸ Come unto me, all ye that Labor and are heavy laden, and I will give you rest. ²⁹ Take my yoke upon you, and learn of me; for I am meek and lowly in heart: and ye shall find rest unto your souls. ³⁰ For my yoke is easy, and my burden is light."

There are progressive steps associated with operating the Laws of the kingdom of God just like there are steps to overriding the natural law of Gravity and, if we are to be successful in accessing the blessing of God, we must know these necessary steps, and execute them in order to receive the blessing of the Kingdom of God.

STEP NUMBER ONE

"Identify!" what you have

Consider Mark 6:32-44; we will see in this portion of scriptures exactly what Jesus did to activate the blessing of God to feeding the multitude. Looking at the disciples, they said to Jesus in verse 35-36; let's send the people away so that they may buy food to eat.

This is a natural response of the disciples, and with our natural mentality when we are faced with financial situations we think we need to work overtime or get a part time job to meet a financial situation, or in this case sending the people away, this the mentality of the kingdom of darkness.

To understand this we need to remember what happen in Genesis 3 when God placed Adam in the garden. He had everything he needed, but when he failed God, the earth was cursed, and the only way that the earth would produce was through sweat meaning man would have to work for it If you think about it mankind went into slavery under the kingdom of darkness with the devil as the god of this world system.

In 2 Corinthians 4:4; this is not saying that we are not working, but rather we must learn how to work the Word of God, the Word of God will work if you work it. This can only be done by applying Romans chapter 12 and verse 2; renewing our minds so that we can live by the Kingdom of God's laws. If we continue to operate by the natural way of doing things we will never break free of the world system (kingdom of darkness).

This is what Jesus meant when He said "Yoke up with me and I will show you how to operate the Kingdom laws so you can experience life in the blessing of God while living here on earth", in other words how to bring the blessing from Heaven to earth. So what did Jesus do? Jesus asked, "What do you have?" and they came back with the answer, "Five loaves and two fish."

Now, in the natural mind "five loaves and two fish" is not a valid answer to the question, "What are we going to feed these *Twenty thousand* hungry people with?" It's not a solution to the problem; it's barely enough lunch for one. Jesus said something that we need to catch. He said, "First, bring it to Me." They did so, and the Bible says He blessed it.

When we as Christians ask God's blessing upon our natural food we are asking God to sanctify and set it apart for the nourishment of our body. (See 1Timothy 4:4-5)

The word blessed means to separate or to consecrate. What was Jesus separating the bread from? Well, legally, remember we're talking about Kingdoms. He was separating the bread from the legal dominion of men and the kingdom of darkness and placing it under the legal dominion of the Kingdom of God and His government.

Then He gave it back to them, but they received it back from Him without realizing that the bread was now in a new Kingdom, under a new jurisdiction of law. Then and only then was the bread able to be multiplied for the feeding of the multitude.

The Bible says let everything be established between two or three witnesses. 1 Corinthians 13:1; let's look at another example of this Kingdom of God law in operations.

According to:

> 1 Kings 17:11-14; "the Widow of Zarephath with the morsel of bread"
>
> 2 Kings 4:1-7; "Elisha Helps a Poor Widow with a little oil".

In these three examples we see that the men of God took something they had and met their situations. My reason for sharing these examples is because God is going to use something that you have to meet a need. So when you have a need in the area of provision, step number one is: Find something you have and sow it into the Kingdom. Seek the Kingdom of God operates by giving and receiving, and the kingdom of darkness operates by buying and selling. Jesus taught continuously about giving in this way.

For example;

> Luke 6:38; (NLT)
>
>> "Give and you will receive. Your gift will return to you in full — pressed down, shaken together to make room for more, running over, and poured into your lap. The amount you give will determine the amount you get back."

STEP NUMBER TWO

"Receive a strategy from the Holy Spirit"

We must be sensitive to the plan of the Holy Spirit. Why is this? Because money is not in Heaven, and if you ask God for money, He cannot rain it down to you because the money you need is in the marketplace.

What the Holy Spirit can do, however, once you give Him the care of your provision, He will show you where it is. By giving you an idea, a plan, a direction, a concept, He can show you how to capture what you need. In this case, Jesus gave them a plan. "Have the people sat down in groups," He said, "and began to pass out the bread."

As Christians we not only need to be born-again, but we must be filled with the Word of God and we must be filled with the Holy Spirit and pray in the Spirit, meaning to speak in other tongues. The Bible says when we speak in tongues we speak to God, and we are speaking mysteries. (See 1 Corinthians 14:2)

Theses mysteries could very well be strategies for a business plan that God wants to give you to generate the money that you are in need of, remember it is not just for you to be blessed, but for you to be a blessing to others. (See example on page 26)

It says: "Don't worry about anything; instead, pray about everything. Tell God what you need, and thank him for all he has done. (Philippians 4:6; NLT) Also, it is important that if you are married that Husband and wife be in agreement, because your prayers can hinder you if you are not. (1 Peter 3:7)

You simply do what Jesus did. The disciples gave what they had to Jesus and He blessed it, and after blessing it He gave it back to the disciples. Lay your hands on your gift, and speak over it. Pray and release it into the Kingdom of God, and in doing this you are taking what you have and placing it under the legal dominion of the government of God.

A) Be Specific - Jesus has destroyed the curse over my life. Christ has redeemed me from the curse of the law. For poverty He has given me wealth. I am prosperous, rich, and wealthy, I am out of debt and all my needs are met. I have plenty more to put in store. I sow bountifully; I reap bountifully. Heavenly Father, like a magnet, I am attracting your blessing, I am full of life, and I am Debt Free. Be <u>very specific</u> about what it is that you are asking for and validate it with a promise from the Word of God. (Matthew 9:19-21)

B) You must be in Faith - "And Jesus answering saith unto them, Have faith in God. For verily I say unto you, That whosoever shall say unto this mountain, Be thou removed, and be thou cast into the sea; and shall not doubt in his heart, but shall believe that those things which he saith shall come to pass; he shall have whatsoever he saith. (Mark 11:22-23) Examine scripture verses where Jesus said their faith has done this or that. (Mark 10:51-52)

C) Release your Faith – by speaking or confessing God Word (blessing), giving your seed and assignment. Therefore I say unto you, what things soever ye desire, when ye pray, believe that ye receive them, and ye shall have them. Mark 11:24. Are you in Faith (Can you see yourself with what you believe that you receive?) (Matthew 8:9-11)

D) Expectation – you must be full of expectation, excitement and joy about your blessing from God.

STEP NUMBER THREE

"Release your faith in God with words and prayer"

Step number three that we need to follow in this story is bringing what we have under the dominion of the Kingdom of God just like Jesus did. You may ask, "Why do I need to do that?" Well, the Bible is clear on this, "Receive a strategy from the Holy Spirit" and you act on the strategy that you receive by faith, and this is done with a believing heart, and a mouth that speaks the promises of God.

Summary

Let me say again, winning in life in any area not only requires spiritual laws and understanding the Kingdom, but it also requires understanding the natural laws and obtaining wisdom in the affairs of life. My life changed by applying the Kingdom of God laws and principles to my situation. The words of Jesus, in Luke chapter four at the beginning of His ministry, Jesus very first words were about the issues of life. He was reading the scroll of Isaiah 61, which contains these words: "The Spirit of the Lord is on Me, because He has anointed Me to preach good news to the poor." Being poor or having a lack of finances is a very important issue of LIFE! (Luke 4:18)

Once you begin to understand the Kingdom of God Laws and Principles and their potential and provision, my friend, you're going to find that it is indeed "Good News."

In order to walk in our inheritance we need to understand these laws and principles of the kingdom and implement them in our lives with clear specific instructions.

Are you ready to Come to Jesus in obedience to Matthew 11:28-30; If yes, on the next few Pages there is a list of scriptures to help you to <u>establish</u> a relationship with the God and become a citizen of the Kingdom through receiving His only begotten Son Jesus who is the Christ.

Decision Page

As I have shared with you about the subject of **Jesus statement..."Come and Learn of Me"** the only way that you can experience and walk in the blessing of God is by receiving the Lord Jesus Christ as your own personal Lord and Savior.

Jesus said "except you are born again, yea shall not see the Kingdom of God" **(John 3:3)**.

If you desire to experience the **BLESSING of God** that were covered in this booklet and in the Holy Bible, you must be born-again in order to qualify to be a partaker of the wonderful inheritance that God has for you in accordance to **Colossians 1:12**.

Are you born again?

Listed are some scripture references that you can check out in the Bible to verify what we are saying. There is a short prayer that you can pray to receive the Lord Jesus Christ as your own personal Lord and Savior, and when you do that, you will be born into the Kingdom of God.

God's Word has the power to literally transform your life, recreate the heart of a person, change how they and secure their eternity.

To receive Jesus Christ as your own personal Lord and Savior

Are you born again? Have you ever received Jesus as your Lord and Savior? If the answer to this question is no, read these scriptures and pray this prayer, agreeing with it and believing it from your heart

John 3:16 "For God so loved the world, that he gave his only begotten Son, that whosoever believeth in him should not perish, but have everlasting life"

Romans 10:9-10, 13 "That if thou shalt confess with thy mouth the Lord Jesus, and shalt believe in thine heart that God hath raised him from the dead, thou shalt be saved. For whosoever shall call upon the name of the Lord shall be saved.

For with the heart man believeth unto righteousness; and with the mouth **Confession** is made unto salvation.

John 14:6 " Jesus said unto him, I am the way, the truth and the life: no man cometh unto the Father, but by me."

Pray this prayer now - Salvation
Dear God,

I want to become a citizen of your Kingdom. I come to you in the name of Jesus, your son. I confess I am a sinner. I believe you sent your son to die on the cross for my sins. I confess with my mouth that Jesus Christ is Lord. Thank you for allowing me to become a Christian; I am translated from the kingdom of darkness to the Kingdom of God. In Jesus' name I pray, Amen!

A genuine born-again Christian, a citizen of the Kingdom of God wants, above everything else, to do the will of God. Don't be ashamed to witness to others and tell them how to become a Christian. Join a Bible believing Church and be water baptized as an act of faith to let the world know you are following Christ's example.

Signed _____

Date _____

If you would like to receive the Holy Spirit, ask the Father in Jesus' name to fill you with the Holy Spirit. Believe you receive when you ask, and begin to speak your new language in faith as God gives it to you.

Pray this prayer now - Receive the fullness of the Holy Spirit

Heavenly Father,

I come to you in faith, believing that Jesus Christ died in my place, for my sins, and arose from the dead. I ask you to fill me to overflowing with the Holy Spirit. You said in your Word that if I asked I would receive, so I ask you now to fill me to overflowing with your precious Holy Spirit. I receive Him now by faith and expect to speak with other tongues as he gives me the utterance. In Jesus' Name, Amen

Endnotes

1. Rediscovering the Kingdom by Dr. Myles Munroe
2. Transform Your Thinking, Transform Your Life by Dr. Bill Winston
3. God's Image of You by Charles Capps
4. The Four Laws of salvation by Global Media Outreach
5. Have You Heard of the Four Spiritual Laws at Campus Crusade for Christ International, Orlando, Florida
6. You're not broke you have a seed by Dr. Leroy Thompson Sr.

About the Author

Pastor James L. Monteria was born again. He was called into the ministry, and ordained by Faith Christian Fellowship, International of Tulsa, Oklahoma. To effectively fulfill the call on his life, he attended Rhema Bible Training Center of Broken Arrow a suburb of Tulsa, Oklahoma where he gained a Diploma in Ministerial Training.

Pastor Monteria received his Bachelors of Science Degree in Business Administration from Saint Paul's College in Lawrenceville, VA. He obtained a Master's Degree in Instructional Education from Central Michigan University, Mount Pleasant, Michigan.

Pastor Monteria has ministered the Word of God for the past 20 years through seminars, church services, Bible studies, Prison Ministries, distributions of his books, CD's and DVD's. Pastor Monteria believes that the Bible is the Word of God, and he is an anointed Pastor and Teacher of the Word of God.

His ministries are a combination of anointed Preaching and Teaching the Word of God; and flowing in the gifts of the Holy Spirit as the lead.

PASTOR J. L. MONTERIA IS AVAILABLE FOR
~SPEAKING ENGAGEMENTS~
~BOOK SIGNINGS~
~WORKSHOPS\CONFERENCES~

YOU MAY CONTACT J L MONTERIA VIA

EMAIL: CLMMINISTRY777@YAHOO.COM

POSTAL MAIL: P. O. BOX 932 CHESTERFIELD, VA 23832

WEBSITE: WWW.CLMPUBLICATION.INFO

www.ingramcontent.com/pod-product-compliance
Lightning Source LLC
Chambersburg PA
CBHW061259110426
42742CB00012BA/1980